Girls' Respect Groups:

An Innovative Program To Empower Young Women & Build Self-Esteem!

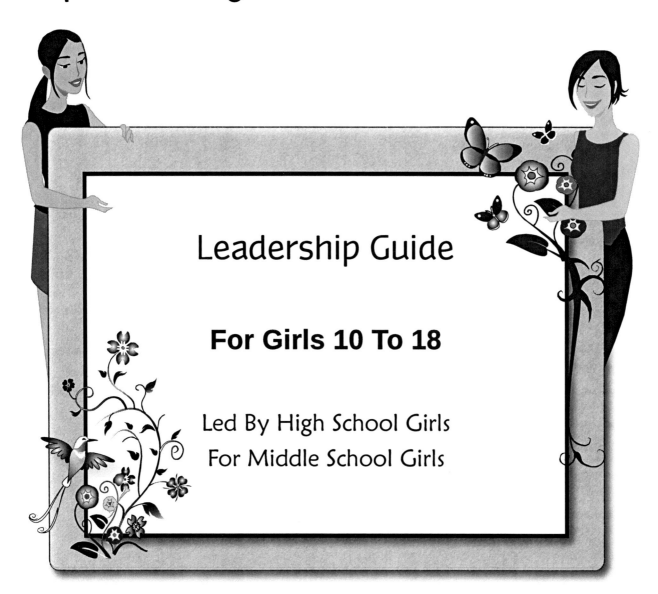

Leadership Guide

For Girls 10 To 18

Led By High School Girls
For Middle School Girls

Lorna Blumen, Natalie Evans, & Anne Rucchetto

Camberley Press

Copyright © 2008 Lorna Blumen, Natalie Evans, and Anne Rucchetto

Publisher Cataloging-in-Publication Data (US)

Blumen, Lorna.
Girls' respect groups : an innovative program to empower young women & build self-esteem / Lorna Blumen, Natalie Evans, Anne Rucchetto.
[ ] p : ill ; cm
Includes bibliographical references.
Summary: Leadership guide and curriculum for high school girls to implement an after-school program for middle school girls.
ISBN: 978-0-9810589-0-0 (pbk)
1. Teenage girls -- Psychology -- Juvenile literature. 2. Teenage girls -- Life skills guides -- Juvenile literature. 3. Self-esteem in adolescence -- Study and teaching (Middle school). 4. Interpersonal relations in adolescence -- Juvenile literature. 5. Respect -- Juvenile literature. I. Evans, Natalie. II. Rucchetto, Anne. III. Title.
158.108352 dc22   BF724.3.S36B686   2009

Library and Archives Canada Cataloguing in Publication

Blumen, Lorna
Girls' respect groups : an innovative program to empower young women & build self-esteem! : Leadership guide / Lorna Blumen, Natalie Evans, & Anne Rucchetto.

Led by high school girls for middle school girls.
Includes bibliographical references.
Interest age level: For girls ages 10 to 18.
ISBN 978-0-9810589-0-0

1. Teenage girls--Psychology. 2. Teenage girls--Conduct of life.
3. Self-esteem in adolescence. 4. Interpersonal relations in adolescence.
5. Respect. I. Evans, Natalie II. Rucchetto, Anne III. Title.

HQ798.B58 2009   158.10835'2   C2009-900892-0

For bulk purchase discounts and other inquiries, please contact www.GirlsRespectGroups.com

All rights reserved. No portion of this book may be reproduced or transmitted without prior written permission of the publisher. This publication is intended to provide informative material and is not a substitute for personal professional services.

All facts, figures, and websites were verified as of January 2009. If you find an error, please contact Camberley Press Ltd at CamberleyPress.com.

References to and reprints from *Respect: A Girl's Guide to Getting Respect & Dealing When Your Line is Crossed,* by Courtney Macavinta & Andrea Vander Pluym, ©2005, are with permission from Free Spirit Publishing Inc.

Cover Design, Interior Design & Layout: Mininder Bath
Design Consultants: Toolbox Creative, ToolboxCreative.com
Photography: Mininder Bath and Gab Gilmour
Illustrations p. 11 & 16: Gurleen Rai

10 9 8 7 6 5 4 3 2 1
Printed in the United States of America

ISBN   978-0-9810589-0-0

Camberley Press Ltd.
PO Box 74553
Toronto, ON M9A 3T0 Canada
CamberleyPress.com

Contents

	Introduction	11
Chapter 1	Why We Need Girls' Respect Groups	19
Chapter 2	What Does A Girls' Respect Group Look Like?	25
Chapter 3	Selecting Girls' Respect Group Leaders	27
Chapter 4	Training Girls' Respect Group Leaders	37
Chapter 5	How To Set Up & Run A Girls' Respect Group	47
Chapter 6	6 Weekly Lesson Plans: Tips For Every Week	57
Chapter 7	GRG Week 1: What Respect Means To Me	67
Chapter 8	GRG Week 2: Your Mind & Your Body	85
Chapter 9	GRG Week 3: Your Media IQ	99
Chapter 10	GRG Week 4: Family	107
Chapter 11	GRG Week 5: Friends & Fighting For Your Rights At School	115
Chapter 12	GRG Week 6: Romantic Relationships, Review, & Wrap Up	125
Chapter 13	Tips For Running Groups Smoothly	137
Chapter 14	Special Situations	141
Chapter 15	Handle This! Awkward Moments & How To Survive Them	143
Chapter 16	Continuing Training & Growth For Leaders	153
Chapter 17	Stay In Touch!	157
Chapter 18	Resources	159

About The Authors

LORNA BLUMEN

is an educational consultant and bullying prevention specialist in Toronto. Her work is solution-focused on children's & teen bullying prevention and the underlying skills needed to solve the problem: respect, conflict resolution, emotional intelligence, stress survival, and resilience.

Lorna runs training workshops for adults who work with children – teachers, parents, school councils, mental health professionals, coaches, and camp counselors. She also works with kids, Grades 1-8, in classrooms, after school programs, camps, & private groups. She mentors high school girls in the Girls' Respect Groups Leadership Program. Her favorite part of GRG is seeing kids step up to their own potential.

She was a contributing author to *When Something's Wrong*, the Canadian Psychiatric Research Foundation's best-selling family handbook. Her chapter "Bystanders To Children's Bullying" was published in *The Art of Followership: How Great Followers Create Great Leaders & Organizations*, Jossey-Bass, 2008.

Lorna has appeared on Canadian local and national TV & radio, at international conferences, and has contributed to articles in national magazines on topics of interest to parents and teachers. Lorna was on Parent Education Network's Board of Directors from 1997-2006. Contact Lorna at www.GirlsRespectGroups.com

NATALIE EVANS

is a Grade 12 student in Toronto and a co-developer of the Girls' Respect Groups after school program. She is passionate about resource sustainability, world food and water issues, women's rights, and respect. Natalie was a 2007 recipient of the Louise Russo Award for community service for her work on bullying prevention with Lorna.

ANNE RUCCHETTO

is a Grade 12 student in Toronto and a co-developer of the Girls' Respect Groups curriculum. She got involved in GRG through her work on bullying prevention with Lorna. Anne loves working with middle school girls and the other great people drawn to the program and plans to stay active in GRG when she goes to university next year.

MININDER BATH
is a social work student at Sheridan College in Oakville, ON. Her background includes a degree in Graphic Communications Management from Ryerson University in Toronto. Min drew on both of those talents in her role as the illustrator of the Girls' Respect Groups Leadership Guide. Min is passionate about empowering the minds of young women. She continues to be an advocate for social change.

A Message From Courtney

When Andrea Vander Pluym and I set out to write RESPECT: A Girl's Guide to Getting Respect & Dealing When Your Line Is Crossed (Free Spirit Publishing, 2005), we had one major goal in mind: to empower girls to build respect from the inside out. And with their Girls' Respect Groups Leadership Guide, Lorna Blumen, Natalie Evans, Anne Rucchetto, and Mininder Bath have done just that! It's a dream come true to see the book inspire a full-fledged program for middle school girls led by high school girls. This is exactly the kind of social change we'd hoped girls would lead after reading RESPECT.

I'm truly honored that the designers of this program have created so powerfully from RESPECT to help its message come alive and live on through the eyes and action of real teen girls. I believe girls are the greatest untapped resource in changing our world for the better by spreading respect. And with this guide, they can use their voices and sisterhood to create the world we all want to live in. A world where each person respects him or herself, creates mutual respect in their relationships and creates social change so all people are respected!

With gratitude and awe, thank you Lorna, Natalie, Anne, & Min for your vision, heart, and hard work.

Much respect!

Courtney

"There is no social change fairy. There is only change made by the hands of individuals"
...Winona LaDuke

Acknowledgments & Thanks

Most of all, the deepest, widest thank you to Courtney Macavinta and Andrea Vander Pluym, whose kind-hearted, encouraging, and inspiring book, *Respect: A Girl's Guide to Getting Respect & Dealing When Your Line Is Crossed*, lit a fire under us to continue their important work. This is truly "it takes a village" work, where each of us benefits from the work and contributions of those who came before. We're not expected to finish the task, but it is our responsibility to contribute. We send this work out in the same spirit, in honor and recognition of those who work hard for girls (& boys), of all ages, everywhere.

An endless round of "thank you"s to Min Bath, my extremely capable assistant and the illustrator of this book. Her creativity and heart brought this manuscript to life. In addition to Min's bottomless knowledge of graphics and printing, her patience, persistence, attention to detail, and good humor were invaluable to the production of this book. Wendy Brookshire's design & manuscript preparation expertise were a huge contribution.

Thank you to Hannah Silverman, whose editing eagle eyes, mother's heart, and publishing experience were a huge help. Thank you for being so generous with your expertise.

Thank you to Carolyn Vranesic, whose experience and empathy as a wonderful teacher, mother, and human being encouraged us and helped us, especially with "Sticky Situations", conflict resolution, and family issues. Thanks also to Chris Fraser, Jenna Chadwick, and Lori Mignone for great ideas and covering details.

We thank our families for their encouragement and enthusiasm. Thank you for making the space and time that allowed us to give our best to this work.

A final thank you to the girls, teachers, and schools where we've run Girls' Respect Groups. Their contributions, "thumbs up"s, and occasional "thumbs down"s, helped us refine and shape this program into what it is today.

"Be the change that you want to see in the world"
... *Mahatma Gandhi*

Introduction

About two years ago, Courtney Macavinta's and Andrea Vander Pluym's beautiful book, **Respect: A Girl's Guide to Getting Respect & Dealing When Your Line Is Crossed**[1] (we'll call it **Respect** from now on), came across my desk. At the time, my work was focused on bullying prevention and conflict resolution skills for elementary and middle school age kids. Surprisingly, I often lecture to adults – parents, teachers, mental health professionals, and camp counselors. That's because **adults, *all of us*, without realizing, are often the root cause of kids' bullying**[2] But that's a different book!

When I lecture or run workshops for adults, I often bring high school students with me. These students stand up and speak for a few minutes about their own experiences with all three bullying roles – the bully, the target, and the bystander. It's a universal experience – we've all played all three roles.

When these bright, articulate young women (for some reason, they've all been women) speak from their hearts about the pain and discomfort they've experienced in each of those roles, adults really "get it". This is a very valuable part of our program, & we have been enriched by the enthusiasm and hard work of these remarkable young women, two of whom became my co-authors of this book.

As part of our frequent discussions, the students wondered about other ways they might help out. **Our talks focused on the perils of middle school, where bullying peaks**[3] **and friendships often suffer**. Preteen girls, in particular, seem to lose their bearings and their stability, for at least a while, during that time. One of these conversations sparked my memory of having recently seen Courtney's and Andrea's book. We started talking about the importance of keeping girls grounded in self-respect and how we might bring this book into use in middle and high schools. Our eyes opened wide around the table and, the next thing we knew, we were working hard to develop the curriculum for this Girls' Respect Groups program.

We've had a great time running & refining the GRG program in schools. As word spread, parents, teachers, & students asked how to find GRG Leaders and run GRGs in their

---

[1] Macavinta, C and Vander Pluym, A. *Respect: A Girl's Guide to Getting Respect & Dealing When Your Line is Crossed.* Minneapolis: Free Spirit Publishing, 2005.
[2] Blumen, L. "Bystanders to Children's Bullying: The Importance of Leadership by 'Innocent Bystanders'". In Riggio, R, Chaleff, I, and Lipman-Blumen, J (eds). *The Art of Followership: How Great Followers Create Great Leaders and Organizations.* San Francisco: Jossey-Bass, 2008.
[3] Coloroso, B. *The Bully, the Bullied, and the Bystander.* Toronto: Harper Collins, 2002.

schools. Now we're thrilled to share it with you! This **Girls' Respect Groups Leadership Guide** will show you how to find & train teen leaders & adult program advisors and run great Girls' Respect Groups in your own communities!

Who's This Book For?

This book is for anyone who's curious about or wants to run a Girls' Respect Group program:

- ☆ **High School Teen Girls** Searching For A Rewarding Volunteer Leadership Experience
- ☆ **Preteen & Middle School Girls** Deserving Healthy, Supportive Friendships
- ☆ **Parents** Raising Self-Confident, Self-Respecting Daughters
- ☆ **Teachers & School Administrators** Building A Respectful School Environment
- ☆ **Mental Health Professionals** Strengthening Girls' Self-Esteem & Decreasing Bullying

Why This Program Is So Special

This program is unique because it is designed to be led by high school young women, under the guidance and supervision of an adult advisor. While many social support programs for girls have adults in key roles as "talking heads", **Girls' Respect Groups puts middle school girls directly in contact with the people they most want to talk to – high school young women.**

The benefits to middle school girls are enormous. Girls' Respect Groups give preteen girls the chance to:

- ☆ Talk openly with high school young women & learn from their experience
- ☆ Build a strong network of supportive girlfriends
- ☆ Talk regularly about important issues & concerns
- ☆ Solve friendship problems with peer & high school mentor guidance
- ☆ Step back & see problems clearly, freed from the "emotional whirlpool"
- ☆ Work to solve problems as they evolve over 6 weeks
- ☆ Stop small problems while they're still small
- ☆ Develop moral strength & peer support to stop gossip & exclusionary behavior
- ☆ Build trust between middle school & high school girls
- ☆ Contact adults easily to intervene early & defuse dangerous problems

What Are The Benefits For The Teen Leaders?

For all the obvious benefits for middle school girls, there are probably *even more* rewards for the high school girls. First and foremost, this program is a great chance for teens to play to their strengths. Girls' Respect Group is a place where leadership-minded young women can really shine. **These high school girls are selected and valued for their specific knowledge and expertise and their unique ability to form a special mentorship connection with preteen girls. Think for a minute about how unusual it is for teens to be offered a job where they are valued and respected for their expertise. Here the *teens* are the experts. This is a job they can do better than anyone else** – and they're not just flipping burgers. We love burgers – as long as they're part of a healthy diet – but *anybody* can flip a burger. As one of our Leaders said, "It's a chance for teens to raise eyebrows for the **right** reasons!"

Great Rewards

It's a beautiful opportunity for high school girls to reach a helping hand back to middle school girls – in support, encouragement, empathy, and mostly, with experience and perspective. It's an amazing chance for these grounded young women to help others in their community who really need it, at a crucial time in their lives. The middle school girls ask questions, get advice, and benefit from the experience of mature, kind-hearted teens. Middle school girls quickly learn that problems which seem overwhelming and insurmountable today virtually vanish by high school, as kids' self-esteem and sense of self solidify. The more secure kids feel about who they are, the less they feel a need to compete with or denigrate others. Risky behaviors diminish, too.

By leading this program, high school young women get a chance to re-evaluate their own relationship with respect and to make changes in all of their important relationships – friends, romantic interests, parents, siblings, teachers, and bosses. **We learn best by teaching, and it's great for our teens to reinforce what they already know about respect**.

While working on this program, one of our teen Leaders mentioned that she'd decided to break up with her boyfriend, who had seemed like a nice guy from the few comments she'd

made previously. In the past month, he seemed to be starting to like another girl, and wasn't being straightforward about it – probably not to himself, either (honestly, lots of much older adults, with much more romantic experience, have found themselves in this situation!). Anyway, she said to us, "I thought to myself, 'How can I hold myself up to these 6th grade girls as someone who understands respect, when I suddenly find myself in a relationship where I'm being treated disrespectfully?'" When I heard her say that, the hairs stood up on my arms! If every girl and woman (and boy and man) can internalize what respect looks like in such an organic, holistic way, so many problems could be stopped at their earliest stages.

GRG Leaders start off great and get even better. Their leadership and group facilitation skills improve with the hands-on experience of organizing and running the GRG after school program. It's not the adults running it – it's the teen Leaders. They have to deal with preteen unruliness, boredom, social dramas, food fights – everything they'll need to learn to enter the adult workplace! Seriously, the teens' group leadership skills take a quantum leap forward.

Finally, **it's a wonderful avenue for community service.** Teens can satisfy their graduation requirement for community service by being Girls' Respect Group Leaders. With community support, high school girls could also be paid for their work, after a certain number of volunteer hours. Monetary payment is a respectful way for adults to honor the girls' expertise, efforts, and commitment.

What's Inside The Girls' Respect Group Program?

Using the **Respect** book as the centerpiece, we have pulled together a diverse array of complementary materials and activities – with lots of time & ideas for open discussion, self-assessment quizzes, games, role plays, video & movie clips, ads, journaling, and much more. We've organized it as a 6 week, 90 min after school program. The program can be used exactly as this book lays out, but we also encourage you to customize it to your own group, add your own materials and make it your own program. Send us an e-mail and let us know how you've taken the program further!

You'll find this GRG Leadership Guide simple to use. The core of the book contains the lesson plans for each of the 6 weeks in the GRG program. There's a lot of useful info on how to select and train high school young women as GRG Leaders,

the logistics of setting up a Girls' Respect Group, even advice on sticky situations and how to deal with them. Everything we've learned from developing and leading this program, we're passing on to you so you can hit the ground running!

Why Run This Group With 6th Grade Girls?

We like the idea of using this **GRG Leadership Guide** and reading the **Respect** book as part of an after school discussion program for 6th Grade girls. It's a great way to reach out and help 6th Grade girls stay strong in their sense of self-respect, respect for others, and be able to ask others to treat them with respect. We want to catch girls early in middle school, before they lose their balance.

It's also a great chance to get to know girls they've never known well before, or to deepen and cement friendships that started in preschool. Many kids, boys and girls, change schools at the start of middle school, and face the challenge of making new friends. Girls' Respect Group is a great way for new kids to join and get connected.

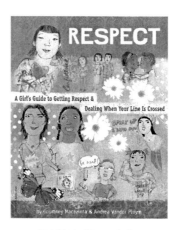

Reprinted with permission
Free Spirit Publishing

Respect (the book) is actually targeted at slightly older girls, both middle and high school levels. There are chapters in the book, about dating and sex, which 6th graders aren't always ready for or interested in. We tell them to hang on to the book because the time will come when they do want to find out more about these things, and they will find the same good ideas and advice about the "yucky romance stuff" of the teen years that they found in the earlier chapters on friendship, family, media influences, etc.

While our goal is to catch and support kids early, it's never too late to use the **GRG Leadership Guide** and read **Respect**. Eighth grade and high school are still valuable times for support and change. We've even given **Respect** to women in their mid-20s who felt the book had something to say to them.

"The future belongs to those who believe in the beauty of their dreams"
... Eleanor Roosevelt

Why An After School Program?

For middle school students with limited transportation options, it's easier to stay after school than to travel to another location for GRG. This creates a challenge for getting the high school girls on-site immediately after their own school day, but we'll talk about that later. Schools with Grades 6-12 in one location make it easy to run GRGs.

The advantages of an after school program, run at school:

- ✪ Girls are already there after school
- ✪ Less driving for parents
- ✪ School is still open (no extra fees to open)
- ✪ Teacher support available
- ✪ Custodial support available (no extra fees)
- ✪ Same location every week

That said, be creative! GRG can be run on weekends or evenings, or as a weekend or vacation retreat. It can be run at school, at community centers, in girls' homes – anywhere adults and teens are willing to come together to create a safe and welcoming space.

Why Just Girls?

No special reason, really. We just happened to find **Respect** at the right time. Boys could definitely use support through the middle school years, too. Boys' friendships, however, are different from girls' friendships. Without being overly general or compartmentalizing, boys'  friendships tend to be focused on activities, on doing things, and less about talking (don't worry, boys talk, too!). Girls' friendships, on the other hand, are more about the quality and connectedness of the relationship itself, with less importance placed on the actual activity. Because of this inherent difference in the nature of the friendships, while Girls' Respect Group is a great program for girls, this type of program, with all the sitting, reading and talking, doesn't get boys deeply interested. We're still looking for good programs for middle school boys. Tell us if you know of any and we'll pass the information on!

The importance of strong connections in girls' relationships is precisely why it's so hurtful to girls to be excluded from relationships, and why Girls' Respect Groups work so hard to change that. The Dalai Lama talks about the need for "warm-heartedness" towards each other. A simple concept with profound results. Lead with a warm heart and the rest will follow. Respect helps us rediscover the warm-heartedness that is in all of us.

Why Not Just Read The Respect Book On Your Own?

Go for it! **Respect** is so beautiful and so helpful, that it's valuable for any young woman to read, whether or not it's part of an organized group. You can use this **GRG Leadership Guide** on your own, too. Courtney Macavinta has an amazing website, **RespectRx.com**, with tons of great info and links to other sites. Check our GirlsRespectGroups.com website, too. You'll be connected into a wider community of girls just by doing that.

There is, however, **a huge benefit to reading Respect and using this Leadership Guide as a group, getting together regularly to discuss ideas. You'll be building a community of supportive girlfriends.** These are friends who will help you and stand by you, friends who understand the corrosive influence of exclusion and back-stabbing, and who will help you stay on a "gossip-free diet" by reminding each other when the conversation veers too far into gossip territory (it takes practice to figure this out and, believe me, adults still make this mistake, too). **You'll build relationships and stay connected to optimistic, strong, supportive, and resourceful friends who will stand by you when it's tough** (and everyone has some tough periods). Like trying to change your eating habits or start a new exercise plan, it really helps to have friends do it with you!

Even if you can't manage to organize a whole after school program, find 1 friend and read **Respect** with her. An older sister might be interested, or even your Mom. Some girls find that reading the book with their Moms opens a window of understanding that can be hard to find during the middle school years. If that's not for you, that's ok, too. Some Moms of girls in our after school groups liked the idea of organizing their own Moms' reading group.

The Circle Widens

Developing this curriculum has fostered so many **connections among women, young women, and girls.** It's been an *amazing* intergenerational collaboration of wonderful women, from ages 10 to 60!

Here's one example: While finding materials on Media Influence (Week 3), we discovered a beautiful video, called "Influences & Identity", posted to YouTube. I e-mailed the creator, telling her how great we thought her video was. I explained what we were doing and asked her if we could use it in the GRG program. She wrote right back, excited that we loved her video! She was a young woman

from Toronto (where the authors live), now away at college (that's "university" to the Canadians out there!). We invited her to come back and participate in some of the GRGs or Leaders training workshops.

A Big Thank You!

We've received so much encouragement and support along the way – from Courtney Macavinta, from the many creators of the additional resources and materials we've examined and included in this program, from preteens, teens & women we've met & worked with along the way, and from our families, who generously supported us while we wrote this book.

We've been so gratified to see the change and growth in every one of us who've been part of this program: middle school participants, high school Leaders, and the adults around them – GRG program advisors, guidance counselors, and teachers. We're excited to get this program out to a larger community – yours! Take this program as a starting point and make it your own. Let us know how you do it!

With love & support for you all,

Lorna   *Natalie*   *Anne*

Lorna   Natalie   Anne

CHAPTER 1
Why We Need Girls' Respect Groups

For at least the past 10 years, 30% of students in the US and Canada have been directly involved in bullying[4] – as bullies, targets, or both. Recent studies, with more precise questions, show much higher rates. Almost 60% of elementary school kids in Canada report being bullied and 50% have bullied others.[5] When you include the activity of (not so) "innocent bystanders", the participation rate nears 100%. Bullying is, shamefully, still a huge problem in schools and workplaces. This is unacceptable & we can do much better!

Prevention is the only remedy for these problems. There will never be enough metal detectors, school suspensions, or armed police in the schools (or society). Mistakes should have consequences, but we need to focus much more on prevention than on punishment.

We think GRGs can help. When people know and respect each other as individuals and as human beings, there is much less intentional bullying. Further, **if girls (& boys) can remain strong and grounded in their sense of self-respect, they'll feel more secure, and will be *more* likely to treat others with respect – less bullying! Kids grounded in respect for *others* will also be less likely to be *bystanders* to bullying.**[6]

Refusing to be a bystander can put a quick end to bullying. Bullying stops in 10 seconds when a bystander intervenes, 57% of the time.[7] Kids must feel confident that they will not be bullied or excluded and also safe to speak up when someone else is.

There are far-reaching benefits. Reducing bullying in schools could improve school dropout rates, too. An estimated 10% of school dropouts do so because of bullying,[8] and 7% of 8th Graders stay home at least once a month to avoid bullies.[9] This needs to stop now!

Confidence

Girls' Respect Groups connect girls to one another. The bonds created by the trust-based GRG curriculum are incredibly strong – between the girls, between the Leaders, and between the girls and Leaders. That said, 6 weeks in a GRG program

---

[4] US Department of Health & Human Services. *Bullying is Not a Fact of Life*. CMHS-SVP-0052, Washington, DC, 2003.
[5] Craig, W, Pepler, D, Jiang, D, and Connolly, J. "Victimization in Children and Adolescents: A Developmental and Relational Perspective", in preparation, prevnet.ca, 2008.
[6] Batsche, G and Knoff, H. "Bullies and Their Victims: Understanding a Pervasive Problem in the Schools". *Psychology Review*, 1994, 23(2), 165-174.
[7] Pepler, D and Craig, W. *Making a Difference in Bullying*. Toronto: York University, arts.yorku.ca/lamarsh, Report 60, 2000.
[8] Weinhold, B and Weinhold, J. "Conflict Resolution: The Partnership Way in Schools". *Counseling and Human Development*, 1998, 30(7), 1-2.
[9] Banks, R. *Bullying in Schools*. Education Resources Information Center (ERIC) Review, ericdigests.org, 2000.

is not a miracle cure. It will, however, **help girls build a strong support network**. Long after the program has ended, GRG "graduates" can influence the school environment, help each other cope with personal problems, and support one another to plan projects and achieve goals:

- ✪ GRG grads can set the tone for the school, softening boundaries between cliques and organizing school & outside functions – dances, fundraisers, class trips, birthday parties, & grad celebrations – with respect and inclusion for all
- ✪ To raise awareness of women's abuse, a GRG graduate can turn to her GRG friends for ideas and assistance, building momentum and support
- ✪ Bullying prevention needs adults to help kids build early social relationships, by teaching respect and mutuality.[10] GRG can help

Girls' Respect Groups plant the seeds for change! Working with small groups of Grade 6 girls, teaching them the "Respect Basics"[11], and supporting them to adopt a respectful outlook on life, we can reach out to the whole community, and with any luck, the world.

It's Only 15 Girls

You may think that running a group with 15 girls will have a negligible effect on the global community. We disagree! Those 15 girls will learn to respect themselves and others, directly and indirectly influencing the people around them. They'll use their self-confidence to end or walk away from a gossip-filled conversation, to refuse to comment on "how ugly that skirt is", or to protect a classmate from bullying. As these girls spread out, to different high schools, camps, universities, colleges, and workplaces, their respectful behavior can affect thousands of people in their **circles of influence**. And that's the effect of *just one* GRG with 15 girls!

We've seen the difference in our GRG participants & especially in our teen GRG Leaders. Being part of GRG actually enlarges your circle of influence. As you grow in strength and solidify your own self-respect, you reach out with confidence to so many more people – peers, adults, and younger kids, too. We hope you'll run many GRGs and that girls who graduate from GRGs will come back as GRG Leaders when they're in high school. Think what awesome leaders they'll be and how huge their circles of influence can be if they start in Grade 6!

---

[10] Pepler, D, Jiang, D, Craig, W, and Connolly, J. "Developmental Trajectories of Bullying and Associated Factors", *Child Development, 2008, 79(2), 325-338.*

[11] Macavinta, C and Vander Pluym, A. *Respect: A Girl's Guide to Getting Respect & Dealing When Your Line is Crossed.* Minneapolis: Free Spirit Publishing, 2005.

Girls Love Girls' Respect Groups

Do girls like GRG? Ask the girls themselves. Just look at the surveys from our 6th Grade participants, at the end of this chapter, and you can see the value of this program! In each weekly lesson plan in this **GRG Leadership Guide** we've included blank surveys for you to use and an overall program survey for the last week. The girls give us valuable insights to keep improving the program. The surveys are another way for the girls to express their creativity. Some groups turned their surveys into artistic masterpieces, with colored markers and expressive drawings. Other groups stuck to "just the facts". Every group has its own personality!

Girls' Respect Groups Affect Boys, Too

Some of the people that GRG girls will encounter and influence will be ... boys! Grounded in self-respect, GRG girls are better able to recognize, set limits for, and encourage respectful behavior in boys. In the same way that GRGs affect girls, these boys will take on a more respectful lifestyle. This is the **good** side of peer pressure! If we help strengthen the respectful views, opinions, & behavior of society's girls, the boys will follow. We fully support boys' efforts to have strong self-respect and respect for others, and believe that Boys' Respect Groups would be a great idea, too.

Why We Need To Act NOW!

A small community of GRG girls can have a huge influence. Like ripples in a pond, the more Respect Groups we create, the more widespread respectful behavior becomes, with profound effects in other areas. **Teaching and encouraging respectful behavior early makes a big difference.** Adults, *just think of the benefits* if you'd had the chance to strengthen your confidence and self-respect at an early age. The preteens we positively affect now will have an easier time in middle school, when bullying peaks.[12] GRG graduates can influence others in their schools and communities, spreading the word about respect, not with lectures, but with everyday actions.

---

[12] Coloroso, B. *The Bully, the Bullied, and the Bystander*. Toronto: Harper Collins, 2002.

Weekly Feedback Surveys

Help Us Improve!

👍 👎

Week 1
What Respect Means To Me

What 3 Things Did You Like Best This Week?
1. We had a good laugh!
2. we could talk about whatever
3. We could be open

Anything We Should Cut? Or Improve?
1.
2. I ♥-ed the class!
3.

Other Comments? Your Ideas Help Us A Lot! Thanks!

Help Us Improve!

👍 👎

Week 2
Your Mind & Your Body

What 3 Things Did You Like Best This Week?
1. How we taked about real life
2. How we taked about media
3. How we shared comments.

Anything We Should Cut? Or Improve?
1.
2. Nothing
3.

Other Comments? Your Ideas Help Us A Lot! Thanks!

Help Us Improve!

👍 👎

Week 1
What Respect Means To Me

What 3 Things Did You Like Best This Week?
1. That you could speak your mind
2. That we could work with partners
3. Food!

Anything We Should Cut? Or Improve?
1. More cheese
2. Same Ham — Bring in meat
3. Better Juice

Other Comments? Your Ideas Help Us A Lot! Thanks!

It wuz good! ♥

Help Us Improve!

👍 👎

Week 1
What Respect Means To Me

What 3 Things Did You Like Best This Week?
1. everyone shared their stories
2. we talked about what respect means to us.
3. reading the book!

Anything We Should Cut? Or Improve?
1. more cheese!
2.
3.

Other Comments? Your Ideas Help Us A Lot! Thanks!

Everything was great

End Of Program Wrap Up Surveys

Survey 1

Girls' Group Wrap Up
Whole Program Comments

1. Overall, I liked Girls' Group
   [X] A lot ___ Pretty Much ___ Neutral ___ No So Much ___ Not

2. What 3 ideas or things did you learn that have been most useful to you?
   Speak up
   Relationships
   Family

3. What activities did you enjoy the most?
   I liked the games, snacks, and conversation.

4. Which activities did you enjoy least?
   I enjoyed everything but the read.

5. How'd You Like...

Activity	Liked It	Didn't Like	Tell Us More – Why?
Ice Breakers	X		
The Book		O	Sometimes no time
Videos	X		
Discussion	X		
Journal			Sometimes no time
Homework		O	Sometimes no time
Snacks	X		
Other Ideas			

6. What Will You Do/Are You Doing Differently Since Starting This Group?
   Speak up. And listen to my guts.

7. What would you tell other girls who want to do this Girls' Group Program?
   That you can trust everybody here and don't be embarrassed.

8. Anything else you'd like to tell us?
   I had a lot of fun. Thanks

Thank You So Much For Making Girls' Group So Great!
Be Strong & Kind
Take Care Of & Support Each Other
Be True To Yourself
Be Proud Of Who You Are, What You've Learned & Where You're Going

We're Proud Of You!

Survey 2

Girls' Group Wrap Up
Whole Program Comments

1. Overall, I liked Girls' Group
   [✓] A lot ___ Pretty Much ___ Neutral ___ No So Much ___ Not

2. What 3 ideas or things did you learn that have been most useful to you?
   media, boys/relationships & speak

3. What activities did you enjoy the most?
   Talking, games, snack & acting

4. Which activities did you enjoy least?
   I liked everything.

5. How'd You Like...

Activity	Liked It	Didn't Like	Tell Us More – Why?
Ice Breakers	✓		
The Book	✓		
Videos	✓		
Discussion	✓		
Journal	✓		
Homework	✓		
Snacks	✓		
Other Ideas	✓		make more time to talk

6. What Will You Do/Are You Doing Differently Since Starting This Group?
   I delt with problems in a different way.

7. What would you tell other girls who want to do this Girls' Group Program?
   It is very helpful. It was fun & we learned so much.

8. Anything else you'd like to tell us?
   I think we need more time to just talk.

Thank You So Much For Making Girls' Group So Great!
Be Strong & Kind
Take Care Of & Support Each Other
Be True To Yourself
Be Proud Of Who You Are, What You've Learned & Where You're Going

We're Proud Of You!

End Of Program Wrap Up Surveys

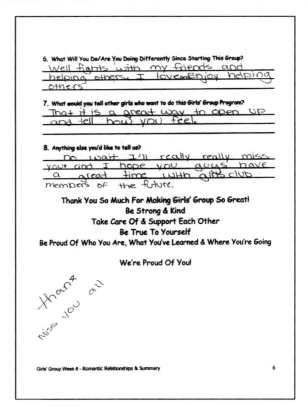

"Never doubt that a small group of thoughtful,
committed citizens can change the world.
Indeed, it is the only thing that ever has"

... *Margaret Mead*

CHAPTER 2
What Does A Girls' Respect Group Look Like?

What does a Girls' Respect Group look like? Put simply, a GRG contains:

- ✭ **2 Female GRG Teen Leaders.** Much more on this later. We have 2 whole chapters on how to find & train these great high school young women!

- ✭ **8 To 16 6th Grade Girls.** Keep the group small enough so everyone gets time to talk. If more than 16 girls are interested, run another group!

- ✭ **1 Or 2 Adult Advisor(s) To The GRG Leaders.** GRG Advisors could be a parent, a teacher, a guidance counselor, or a community leader.

- ✭ **1 6th Grade Teacher Contact From The School.** This teacher will make sure the school's responsibilities get handled smoothly.

Here are a few things to keep in mind:

6th Grade Girls. It's best if all the girls are **from the same school, but not all from the same set of close friends**. A real benefit of GRG is that the problems and issues you discuss are of immediate relevance to the girls – they're living those issues in their daily lives and friendships. Having the opportunity **and** a safe place to discuss & work through these problems improves the girls' friendships and problem solving skills, inside **and** outside of GRG, back in the school environment. While a group of girls from the same school is ideal, it's also great to run a mixed group at a camp, community center, or friend's house.

GRG Adult Advisor(s). GRG Advisors deal with the planning and logistics behind GRG. If you're new to organizing or working with groups like GRG (and even if you aren't), we suggest having 2 advisors to share the work and ideas. Advisors also attend GRG meetings, taking notes and working with Leaders afterwards to decide what works well and what can be improved. Adult Advisors are typically required to attend GRG meetings, as an adult safety person. With the tight scheduling between the end of the Leaders' high school day and GRG's after school start time, Adult Advisors often play a vital role in transporting Leaders. It's very helpful if at least 1 Adult Advisor has a flexible work schedule.

Adult Advisors are crucial to the success of your GRG chapter. There's a fair bit of work involved – especially if there's only 1 Advisor – but it's one of the most inspiring and rewarding projects you can ever work on and is **so** worth the extra effort. **The Adult Advisor really gets the ball rolling for GRG.** Even when the idea to run a GRG comes from the 6th Graders or the teen Leaders, nothing moves forward until the 1st Adult

Advisor steps in. It takes a special person to be a GRG Adult Advisor. **You must really enjoy working closely with teens** (perhaps not your own teen – we get it!), offering mentorship, guidance, and the chance to scaffold a teen leader into her best self, helping bring out the best in young girls coming up behind her (just like you're doing, too!).

The Adult Advisor could actually be a high school teacher, especially to get a new GRG going. In his or her role as start-up Advisor, the teacher could then find a parent or a community leader (or 2) to step into the permanent role of Adult Advisor. A teacher could easily be a 2nd or back up Adult Advisor, especially if he or she can leave right after school ends and head out to the middle school with the teen Leaders on days when there's a GRG running.

Please remember, **it's actually the teen Leaders who are running the group, NOT the adults.** Nonetheless, adults must be present at the meetings, while balancing the need to maintain an open and welcoming environment in which the girls feel comfortable to talk. You can find more on privacy and safety issues later in the book.

6th Grade Teacher Contact. It's essential to have a teacher from the middle school who will be the main GRG contact. The Teacher Contact's first role is to identify the Grade 6 students who will participate in GRG. He or she will also coordinate the flow of parent information and permission slips, and make sure school resources are made available (e.g., the room, A/V needs, snack, custodial support, payments, etc.).

CHAPTER 3
Selecting Girls' Respect Group Leaders

You may be thinking that you, or someone you know, would make a great Girls' Respect Group Leader. You may be right! Let us share with you what we've found to be good qualities and talents to look for in a candidate.

Our Leaders are the most important ingredient in GRG. They make the material come alive! Even more important, our Leaders provide a very human example of respect to the 6th Grade girls in front of them. Today's world is full of bullying, criticism, negative media images, and disrespect. GRG Leaders provide living, breathing examples of how it is possible to have fun and be cool, while being respectful of your friends and encouraging the best in each of us.

The ideal starting age for GRG Leaders is Grade 10. Grade 9 girls (& boys) have a lot on their plates, and aren't yet settled into themselves as teens. A year of high school will make a big difference in maturity and their ability to lead groups and be inspiring role models. Selecting and training GRG Leaders in Grade 10 gives girls the longest time to remain Leaders. They will mature into fabulous Leaders by Grade 11, and even when they get super busy in Grade 12, with college and university applications and work, they can still participate on a reduced basis. Local college students might make good Leaders but, no kidding, they might be too old (too far from 6th Grade)!

Who Are Good Candidates To Be GRG Leaders?

With GRG comes an **exciting and inspiring opportunity for high school Leaders to have a positive, anchoring, supportive influence on middle school girls. We cannot overstate how significant this is.** The girls in Grade 6 want so much to be like the high school girls, that having great role models as Leaders can have an enormous impact. Once Leaders appreciate the strength of their influence, they understand the power of their behavior – even the smallest offhand words, facial expressions, and reactions. GRG will have a ripple effect on all the girls in the group and on the surrounding school community. Choose positive, enthusiastic, inquisitive teens as Leaders and your training is halfway done!

Not surprisingly, a GRG Leader must be a good leader. A Leader is strong, motivational, open to new ideas and people, great at problem solving, and confident, without taking herself too seriously. She must be open to discussing and learning from her past mistakes. She should have a good combination of intelligence and common sense, have strong morals and integrity, be focused on the future, and have a positive outlook on life.

Before you think that we're looking for perfect superstars, let's have a reality check. All these qualities may not be shining through in every applicant. What we're looking for is **possibility and raw material** and a teen who wants the opportunity to learn! It takes a lot of development and practice to run one of these groups, both on the part of the GRG Leaders and their Adult Advisors. We need to give each other space to grow.

We're not perfect, either. It's taken us nearly 3 years of training and running Girls' Respect Groups, including writing and refining the program several times, to feel that we are well-trained Leaders. If you are a young woman who wants to help the next generation of girls coming up behind you, you're special in your own right and you'll make a positive difference, even in your early days as a Leader. In the process, you'll grow a lot.

We want Leaders who believe strongly in empowering young girls and in the strength of sisterhood. Your past experience with the topics we'll discuss in GRG, especially disrespect issues, is the best qualification of all. Your own voice of experience allows you to "walk the talk" as a Leader and to be an authentic role model for the girls. Any teen wishing to run a GRG must respect herself and those around her. If you read **Respect** and still feel you have a lot to learn, it may be better to wait a while, and make some changes within yourself, before you try to teach other girls about respect. We respectfully invite you back when you're ready!

GRG Leaders need to show confidence in themselves and their beliefs, even when it seems "easier" to look the other way. Leaders demonstrate, with their stories and actions, that it is strong to stand up for your own convictions, and with the supportive help of your GRG friends around you, it's also safe.

Why Girls Leading Girls?

Maybe you haven't guessed yet, but we're looking for young **women** to lead our Girls' Respect Groups (sorry, boys!). **Teen leadership brings something really special and unique to GRG.** Teen Leaders have a deep understanding and empathy because they've just lived through what the middle school girls are going through right now. For modeling and teaching girl power, self-respect, and equal treatment, it makes sense to have girls teaching girls.

Middle school girls are very open to the experience of having teen girls as their leaders, more so than with an adult leader (although there are many lovely adult leaders & great adult-led groups). **GRGs connect these two groups of young women, in a win-win for all.** This **GRG Leadership Guide** gives you the "recipe" for how to cook up a great girls' group and facilitate a rewarding connection between awesome, strong teen girls and developing middle school girls. Providing experience and support, teen Leaders are backed up by their Adult Advisors.

Most preteen girls are more comfortable being open with other girls at this time of life. Some may feel awkward around boys at this hormone-dazzled developmental stage. It's extremely important that the girls feel comfortable in the GRG group setting, so they can get the most out of the discussions and activities, many of which encourage opening up and sharing. If the girls aren't relaxed and confident in their group situation, they may miss out on the full experience.

Why Two Leaders?

Working with a partner is an extremely helpful way to split the work of leading a Girls' Respect Group. Being a GRG Leader requires preparation for each meeting, thinking ahead about potential rough spots or awkward questions, preparing handouts and materials, and maintaining the flow of discussion during meetings. The Leaders' cooperation that goes into planning and running GRGs also provides a solid example of respect and teamwork, something we are trying to teach the girls in the first place.

The two Leaders must respect and appreciate each other for their separate areas of experience, and be able to let each other take leading roles for GRG activities. As strange as this may sound, **we recommend that Co-Leaders not be good friends beforehand**. If the Leaders are too close, inside jokes and personal stories could limit the group's discussions, or make the participants feel left out. Even more important,

Know Yourself 1st

Here's a little self-quiz to get you started. Rank yourself from 1-10 on each trait. Be honest, no one sees this but you.

Are You:	Not So Much									That's Me!
Ambitious	1	2	3	4	5	6	7	8	9	10
Assertive	1	2	3	4	5	6	7	8	9	10
Cautious	1	2	3	4	5	6	7	8	9	10
Creative	1	2	3	4	5	6	7	8	9	10
Domineering	1	2	3	4	5	6	7	8	9	10
Eloquent	1	2	3	4	5	6	7	8	9	10
Encouraging	1	2	3	4	5	6	7	8	9	10
Fun Loving	1	2	3	4	5	6	7	8	9	10
Generous	1	2	3	4	5	6	7	8	9	10
Helpful	1	2	3	4	5	6	7	8	9	10
Impulsive	1	2	3	4	5	6	7	8	9	10
Independent	1	2	3	4	5	6	7	8	9	10
Listener	1	2	3	4	5	6	7	8	9	10
Loyal	1	2	3	4	5	6	7	8	9	10
Moody	1	2	3	4	5	6	7	8	9	10
Nervous	1	2	3	4	5	6	7	8	9	10
Open-Minded	1	2	3	4	5	6	7	8	9	10
Problem Solver	1	2	3	4	5	6	7	8	9	10
Sociable	1	2	3	4	5	6	7	8	9	10
True To Yourself	1	2	3	4	5	6	7	8	9	10

Next, write in the margin beside each trait whether you feel that trait is a positive or negative leadership trait (use + or -). Compare your rankings to the pluses and minuses. Do you look like a good leader? Are you perfect? Of course not. Being a GRG Leader is also a chance for you to grow. You can decide whether you're ready to step into the GRG leadership challenge now, or do you have a semester (or more) of growing to do before you're ready to step in and help out?

having 2 Leaders with different backgrounds, experiences and viewpoints really adds richness and diversity to the group.

It's great for the Leaders to have different opinions and even disagree with each other. What better way to demonstrate ways to share viewpoints and disagree **respectfully** with one another? For similar reasons, it helps if the Leaders went to different middle or elementary schools. That way, the Leaders will bring a wider range of experiences, stories, friendships, and views. Believe us, even if you didn't know your Co-Leader previously, once you've run a GRG or 2 together, you will become tight friends and have a lot to talk (& laugh) about! Over time, as you develop a larger group of Leaders, it makes sense to pair a really strong Leader with a new or less experienced Leader.

To prepare for each group meeting, Leaders should divide the week's activities, sharing responsibility for leading at different times. Another advantage of this approach is that **while 1 Leader is leading, the other Leader can be more of an observer.** This is very useful for after-meeting debriefings about which activities ran well and which need more work, observations about the needs of participants, and the social structure of the group.

Where To Look For Leaders

It's most organic to **select high school Leaders from the same community where the GRGs will be run.** The Leaders will have had experience at the "feeder" middle schools, so they can relate to the girls. Plus, it's a great chance to make a difference right in our own communities! **Start by calling local high schools.** Guidance counselors will know the girls with good leadership potential and those involved in leadership activities in the school and in the community. Gym and health teachers are good sources (they're often great Adult Advisors, too!). Check with coaches of school and community sports teams for candidates. GRG Leadership training can be a great high school after school club, too (see Chapter 4)!

If you're a parent of teens, your own child might want to become involved (Or not! That's ok, too), or some of their friends might be great leader candidates. Talk to other parents of teens.

Community centers are an amazing place to find teen girls working as leaders. If they work or volunteer at a community center, they already have great experience. Lifeguards, dance instructors, camp counselors, team sports players, teen coaches of little kids' teams, and peer tutors can all be found at community centers. Girls involved with these activities have great potential for leading a GRG.

Obviously, once you've got a GRG program up and running, your best source of leaders will be referrals from your existing Leaders. They've probably been talking about GRG to their friends and created a lot of interest already. Keep in mind: just because someone is your good friend doesn't guarantee that they would be a good GRG Leader. Don't do this just to have something to do with your friends (although you might be very surprised at how engaged you get!). Look for friends who are already putting themselves out there or have a demonstrated interest in community service. Choose a girl who has what it takes to lead a GRG.

Down the road, your GRG participants will make excellent Leaders. Keep in touch with them. An e-mail list is a great place to start (be sure to get parents' permission). We've started an online network for our "graduates".

The Importance Of Self-Respect In GRG Leaders

GRG Leaders must have that special quality that really makes a person shine and stand out in a crowd. You'll know it when you see it. This secret ingredient is **self-respect!** In GRG, Leaders will be looked at under a middle school microscope (in the nicest possible way). It's important that the younger girls can see and understand what

respect means just by looking at the Leaders. Leaders should be articulate in expressing their opinions, while open to new ideas shared by others. They should be open to questions about themselves, with respectful privacy limits. The GRG setting should be a safe and welcoming space, where young girls, always looking for answers, can ask their questions, feeling secure and respected. It is extremely important that GRG Leaders do not have the "dumb to ask, cool to ignore" attitude, which causes problems with respect from the start.

Pick young women you would be proud to have as role models under the close inspection of younger girls. Look for teens who are good examples in their own relationships with family, friends, and romance. Are we looking for smooth sailing *24/7*? Of course not. *Everyone* has occasional relationship conflicts, *especially* through the drama-filled teen years, where "occasional" is more like "daily". It's more *the way* the teens speak about their friends and parents, and *particularly* the way they describe how they solve their conflicts, that can reveal a thoughtful and mature "relationship manager". Listen for the way they discuss their *mistakes*, what they've learned, and what they do differently now or will in the future.

Leaders who don't listen to others' concerns, or don't take problems seriously, will set a poor foreground for a Girls' Respect Group and could leave the participating girls feeling unimportant and their concerns trivialized. You may find a girl in GRG who is being mistreated and disrespected by her peers outside GRG, sometimes by her own circle of "friends". A girl like this is in a lot of pain at being ignored, excluded, and made the butt of jokes. Sometimes, that's why she joins a GRG. For a GRG Leader to dismiss her problems and concerns, or treat them trivially, would be a huge let-down for a young girl. GRG Leaders are not expected to solve these problems with a magic wand. They *should* listen respectfully, with empathy, be able to provide encouragement, some ideas, and know when the problem needs an adult's intervention.

A GRG Leader can successfully show young girls that it's cool to listen to and appreciate your friends – a huge leap in the right direction. If you're looking for a GRG Leader or looking to become one yourself, listen for signs the potential Leader is willing to listen to what *everyone* has to say, not just her closest or coolest friends.

Don't stress out looking for the superhuman teenage girl. We all have a long way to go. Don't underestimate people's potential. Being involved in GRG is a great way to open someone's eyes and change her life! Looking for the potential greatness in people is what GRGs are all about.

Myth: A GRG Leader Must Be Outspoken, "Popular", Or An Academic Star

Loud, outspoken girls are often thought to be well-respected and good leaders among their peers. This is frequently **not** so. A girl's insecurity can sometimes lead to attention-seeking behavior that people misconstrue as leadership. A quiet girl, often overlooked, can actually have more self-respect and respect among her peers. She doesn't need to be the center of attention to know her own self-worth. So when you're looking for a GRG Leader, be sure to look at all types of girls. Introverted, extroverted, dark-haired, light-haired, intellectually smart, street smart, big, or small, they likely have amazing potential and individually excellent leadership skills. Please don't limit Leaders to the stereotype.

Respect ~~Popularity~~ Makes The Leader

Remember, Girls' Respect Group isn't about being perfect, leading a perfect life, or knowing everything. Leaders can be found in girls who may not fit the conventional picture, but still show leadership potential, personal power, and talent. Leadership extends beyond "the usual suspects" with awesome academic qualifications, sports trophies, and a spotless record. Girls' Respect Group is about giving everyone a chance. Through leading GRGs and developing this curriculum we've learned so much about ourselves. We've become better people along the way.

Other factors demonstrate a teen's willingness & ability to shoulder the responsibility of being an inspiring role model and an effective GRG Leader. Leaders must show their commitment & maturity by attending **all** GRG Leader training sessions, all GRG meetings, preparing for the meetings, and knowing & embodying the **Respect** book & its ideas. GRG Leaders, like all human beings, must be accountable, and if we do mess up (and we all do), we must be ready to take responsibility and make it right.

GRG Leader Candidate Interviews

We think it's good to have 1 or 2 informal interviews with each candidate, to help you pick the best fit for the training program. Some GRG Leadership training programs start as after school clubs. Be flexible about how to conduct interviews.

Keep it casual & low key. Take the candidate out for a snack and conversation. A 30 min relaxed conversation will give you a great sense of whether you're all on the same page. The interview team can be the GRG Adult Advisor and, if available, a GRG Leader. There's a real benefit to having 2 people on the interview team. You will each see different things and see things differently.

Here's a simplified interview process. Customize as needed!

- ✡ **Start by describing GRG and your own experiences with it.** Be positive, enthusiastic, and realistic. Talk about the benefits to the Leaders, to the girls, to the community. If a Leader is part of the team, talk about your own experience of becoming and being a Leader.

- ✡ **Next, learn more about your candidate.** It'll help you compare the candidates if you ask them the same questions. Make a list of 4-6 questions, mostly open ended, so each candidate has a chance to talk about herself, her experience, her values, and why becoming a GRG Leader interests her.

  Sample questions might include:

  1. Why are you interested in leading Girls' Respect Groups?
  2. Describe your past experiences that have prepared you to lead a GRG.
  3. What are your best skills?
  4. What are your worst?
  5. What else would you like us to know about you?
  6. What else would you like to know about us?

  Keep it casual and friendly. You might want to send the question list to the candidates before the meeting, so they can focus their thoughts.

- ✡ **Review the time commitments and dates for training and running your GRG Groups.** Review your decision date and when you'll let her know if she has been selected for training. Thank the candidate for her time and interest, and that's it!

Remember: Not everyone does well in a talking interview, but GRG Leaders have to be pretty comfortable talkers & pretty good listeners, too. They're going to be talking & listening (& thinking) a lot during the 6 weeks of GRG. We recommend picking Leader candidates who seem comfortable and relaxed in the talking interview setting, even, and perhaps *especially,* when they don't have all the answers. Don't forget about those less-skillful talkers, though. See if you can find them behind-the-scenes jobs helping GRG while they grow into comfortable front-men (women!).

> "Your vision will become clear
> only when you look into your heart"
> … Carl Jung

Your Reputation Matters To Us

We care about who leads Girls' Respect Groups. We want to encourage and enable strong female leaders for the future. The beauty of GRGs is that they provide a cross-generational chain of support, starting with the GRG Adult Advisor & Teacher Contact, down through the GRG Teen Leaders, and continuing on to the 6th Grade girls. Girls' Respect Groups are intended to help girls keep in touch with their real, true selves as they grow, so it's essential that GRG Leaders are strong, positive young women who are invested in these principles themselves.

We want you to run the best GRGs possible. We offer you the benefit of our knowledge and experience, to make your GRGs run professionally, with great success. We hope that you, as future Leaders, lead your Girls' Respect Groups to amazing accomplishments.

Girls' Respect Groups, however, are just the beginning. As we said, 6 weeks of GRG, fabulous as it is, will not miraculously change your life or the lives of the participants. What it **will do** is open a window of opportunity, a way of thinking and behaving that is **up to you and your friends to continue, long after GRG has ended**. This is true for both GRG Leaders and participants. The best part of GRG is that it helps form a group of supportive friends around you, to help you keep walking the Girls' Respect walk. You'll want to **make it your personal goal to keep a strong sense of respect for others and yourself, keep learning, and keep reaching out to help others.** This will help you become your best self and it also sets a great example for everyone you encounter in life.

A Note About Safety & Security. Please be mindful of safety concerns when working with children's programs. As a GRG representative, when you introduce yourself to a 6th Grade Teacher Contact or school Principal, be sure to include relevant information about your professional or academic life and general trustworthiness. Please research and comply with your community's requirements, including background checks, for teachers, adult advisors, or teen leaders before they work with middle school students.

"If you want to be respected, you must respect yourself"

... Spanish Proverb

CHAPTER 4
Training Girls' Respect Group Leaders

You've got yourself some great candidates for GRG Leaders. Maybe you're an excellent candidate. Now what? Time for training! Leaders' training for Girls' Respect Groups brings all Leaders to a consistent level of knowledge & familiarity with the material and makes each Girls' Respect Group the highest quality possible.

GRG Leadership training has 2 stages. Stage 1 is Group Training, where Leader candidates meet together, typically for 10-12 weekly sessions. Stage 2 training is "in the field", where teams of 2 Co-Leaders run a 6-week GRG after school program for 6th graders. When you've completed both stages, you'll be a well-prepared GRG Leader!

This chapter outlines Stage 1 Group Training, which has 5 major objectives:

1. Familiarize Leaders with the **Respect** book, this **GRG Leadership Guide**, & the weekly lesson plans for the GRG after school program

2. Improve Leaders' group facilitation skills

3. Build teams of Co-Leaders

4. Practice handling emotional or difficult situations with grace, kindness, & tact

5. Give Adult Advisors a chance to see the teens' personalities in a relaxed environment

We've laid out the big blocks of training content. Feel free to customize – set it up to run the way that works best for you. Let us know your best training tips!

Training Team

The training team consists of the Adult Advisor(s) plus 2-16 teen girls. If Leaders' training is done at a high school, there is usually 1 high school teacher who's the GRG Leadership Training Advisor, plus 1 or more Adult Advisors to help support the GRGs running in the middle schools.

There should be a minimum of 1 Advisor for every 8 teens. We suggest having 2 Advisors, even for 8 teens, especially if the Advisors are new to this type of work. The more adult and experienced trainers the better, because some of your best opportunities to observe the candidates come in the relaxed moments between activities and at break times. Later, when you have trained some Leaders and run some groups, use your experienced GRG Leaders. They will become your best trainers.

Training: When To Start & How Long It Takes

It takes about 24 hours of training before high school girls are ready to lead GRGs. We feel it's worth every minute of effort, & you will, too, when you see the effect it has on the new Leaders, the 6th Grade girls, and the entire community around these young women. It's not a magic wand, but it has amazing results. There are several ways to run GRG training:

- **2 Weekend Intensive Training Sessions, With Four 7-Hour Days** (24 hours of training, with breaks). There will be 1 hour of homework each evening. That's why we call it intense!

- **4 Weekly 7-Hour Training Sessions.** Most of a Saturday or Sunday, for 4 weeks

- **After School Leadership Club.** Meet for 2 hours weekly, after school from September to mid-January, as you prepare to run GRGs starting late January

- **Winter & Spring Training In Preparation For Running GRG Summer Camp.** Start in January. Spring break's a great time to accelerate training, if enough people are available. Work hard in the morning & go to the movies in the afternoon!

S–P–R–E–A–D I–T O–U–T. We really prefer the longer training options. Less pressure, more learning. An important part of training is for each teen girl to co-lead at least one of the weekly lesson plans. With 4 or more consecutive sessions, girls have a chance to prepare (by themselves & with their Co-Leaders) for their leading opportunity. **It also takes a certain amount of time to digest and assimilate the material.** That said, everyone's busy, and the longer training spreads out, the more likely there will be a scheduling conflict with sports tournaments or major school assignments. Schedule the training sessions according to the needs of your group. Everything in life needs a little compromise and balance!

There's another reason to take it slow. A lot of the "training" is the familiarity the Leaders develop with the material *over time*. The larger your training group, you'll find the girls reach readiness to lead at differing times, in clusters. Spread out the training to minimize the intensity and maximize the learning. Run Stage 1 Leaders' training throughout the fall, then start your 1st GRG in mid-January.

Experienced Leaders can start the October groups. **October is the best time to start GRGs for 6th Grade. It catches kids at the beginning of the year** (but they've been there long enough to find their lockers & the bathroom!). It really **gets things off to a good start and sets the respect tone for the whole middle school experience.** That said, we've run great groups till late spring!

To organize GRG leadership training as a high school after school club, set it up with the school Guidance Office or one of the teachers. Attend Club Sign Up Day. Make a poster & a 1-page flier describing **Respect** & the GRG Leadership Training Program. To get you started, see our sample flier, "*Calling All Grade 10 Girls!*", at the end of this chapter. (Note: Download this and other materials at our **GirlsRespectGroups.com** website). When you have trained GRG Leaders, they can recruit friends and make fliers, too. Contact us for ideas or help – we keep posting new training materials. Send us your best & we'll pass them on!

Materials

Every Adult Advisor and Leader-in-Training will need:

- A copy of **Girls' Respect Groups Leadership Guide** (this book)
- A copy of **Respect**
- A blank journal
- A 2-pocket folder
- A pen or pencil
- Water bottle (girls bring their own)
- Snacks & water refills (see below)

Before Stage 1 Training Begins

Ask Leader candidates to **read Respect**, **cover to cover**, making notes or highlighting their favorite parts and ideas they disagree with. Focus on the Intro and Chapters 1, 2, 3, 4, 5, 6 & 11, the chapters covered in the 6 week GRG program. Read the **GRG Leadership Guide,** Intro, and Chapters 1-4. This will give Leaders-in-Training a good sense of the goal – *and soul* – of this program. Remind the teens to bring their books to **every** training session. Trainers should review this material, too.

Cost

Each group needs to make its own decision about who pays for the cost of Leaders' training. We suggest that the teens buy their own copies of **Respect** & the **GRG Leadership Guide**. It's a way of expressing investment in the program. GRG Advisors can do the ordering. There are several options for funding the remaining materials:

- Adult Advisors can pay for the rest of the supplies
- The high school can pay

- ✰ Government or private foundation grants can be sought. Applications are very time-consuming for the small amount needed, unless you've organized a multi-year training schedule
- ✰ Leaders-in-Training or parents can contribute $20-30 towards snacks & materials
- ✰ Community service agencies (eg, Kiwanis or Rotary) often fund similar activities

Please make sure consideration and financial support are given to teens who may not have the money for materials but would make great Leaders!

Stage 1 Training Overview

Stage 1 Training should cover these topics. GirlsRespectGroups.com has a Stage 1 Weekly Training Agenda you can download.

- ✰ **Introductions.** Games & icebreakers for getting to know you. Alternate kinetic games with talking around the table. Get-to-know-you questions can include:
    - ☑ Why are you interested in leading Girls' Respect Groups?
    - ☑ What previous experience prepared you for leading a GRG?
    - ☑ What are your future plans & interests? (we know these will change)
- ✰ **Hand Out A Journal & 2-Pocket Folder For Each Leader-In-Training.** The journal is for notes & assignments. Ask the teens to spend 5 min after each session (more if they like) describing their highlights or 3 favorite activities of the day and their insights, especially how they might be seeing things differently after attending "Respect Boot Camp"! The folder keeps the paperwork organized.
- ✰ **In-Depth Review Of Respect, Chapter 1: *"What Respect Means To You"*.** Go around the table and ask each teen to pick her favorite of the *7 Respect Basics*. Make sure to cover all 7 Basics. Ask what the *7 Respect Basics* look like in real life (both for Grade 6 & high school). Ask for real life examples from the teens and Advisors. If the group is large, you can split up into 7 smaller groups to talk about the *7 Respect Basics*, then return to the larger group where each team "presents".
- ✰ **Review & Practice The 6 Weekly GRG Lesson Plans.** Assign teams of 2 Leaders-in-Training to present 1 lesson plan to the group. Spread it out – don't do all 6 weeks back-to-back in 1 afternoon! If you're doing a "marathon" weekend training, do Weeks 1, 2, & 3 in the afternoon on Day 1 and Weeks 4, 5, & 6 on Day 2. Do 1 Lesson Plan per week for weekly training.
- ✰ **Leaders' Training Feedback.** It's helpful to give each Leader-in-Training some kindhearted feedback along the way, both in her role as Leader (when she's

leading a weekly Lesson Plan) and as Participant (for the other days or weeks when she's *participating* in someone else's Lesson Plan leadership practice). Leaders-in-Training should be reviewed by the Adult Advisors and Senior GRG Leaders running the training program AND also by themselves. We've included sample feedback forms for both the Leader & Participant role at the end of this chapter.

Keep the feedback simple, gentle, & encouraging. Build on her strengths, while kindly suggesting where she needs to grow & improve. Did she fully cover the material in the Lesson Plan? Did she use the **Respect** book effectively? Did she share leadership with her Co-Leader? Encourage group participation? Listen well, with empathy? Contribute her own (appropriate) stories to add interest to the Lesson Plans? Encouraging feedback, given early & often, helps Leaders-in-Training grow into their full potential.

✡ **Homework.** Homework is most intense for the 1-Weekend Training, so we'll give you the most guidance here. **Homework after Day 1** is for everybody **not** presenting on Day 2. Review Weeks 4, 5, & 6 before Day 2. **Leaders who will be presenting on Day 2** should work with their Co-Leaders to prepare. Spend 30 min reading & thinking about your lesson plan. Then have a 15-30 min phone call with your Co-Leader (exchange phone numbers!), to discuss ideas and divide up activity leadership.

✡ **Homework For Longer Training Programs**. Same basic idea: keep reading from **Respect** and prepare with a Co-Leader to lead lesson plans from the **GRG Leadership Guide**, just do it at a gentler pace!

✡ **Partnership & Co-Leading Opportunities**. Look for ways to have the teens work together in pairs over the course of the training sessions. Presenting to the group will be good practice and a good opportunity for the Adult Advisors to assess the teens' facilitation skills. As we suggested, the **Respect** Chapter 1 review can be used this way, dividing the teens into pairs to discuss and present the *7 Respect Basics*. By the end of training, you should be able to tell which teens are strongest or most experienced. Pair them with a Co-Leader who's a little less strong. Make sure these partnership pairs have a chance to do some group activities together to test out their partnership style.

Role Play: "Awkward Situations"

Training Girls' Respect Group Leaders

- ✦ **Healthy Snacks & Water.** A big healthy snack is an essential part of this program, both for the Leaders' training and for the eventual GRG after school program. You'll read more later about our commitment to the value of healthy snacks! Healthy food gives teens (& adults) more energy, brain ability, and stamina. For the 9-hour sessions, plan on 2 meals & 1-2 small snacks. For the 6-hour sessions, you'll need 1 meal & 1 snack, or 2 meals, depending on the timing. You can't go wrong with large, frequent, healthy snacks for teens. Remember to serve lots of water. Ask the girls to bring their own reusable water bottles.

- ✦ **Facilitation Skills. Cover the later chapters of the GRG Leadership Guide – tips for running smooth groups & handling special situations.** Role play some "Awkward Moments". Make up more of your own. These are good to use as kinetic breaks from sitting. Practice makes us professional.

- ✦ **Icebreakers.** You can never have enough icebreakers. There are whole books devoted to icebreakers – talking games, percussion games, twist-yourself-into-a-pretzel-then-untwist games! See the list of icebreakers in our Resources chapter. Pick your favorites, or make up new ones. Give the teens a list of 20 icebreakers for "energy-lull emergencies". Part of training homework could be for everyone to bring 1 icebreaker to Day 2. That's the start of your list of 20! Send us your favorites!

- ✦ **Review Chapter 5 Of The GRG Leadership Guide: How To Set Up & Run A GRG.** Even though a lot of the work in setting up the GRG will be the Adult Advisor's responsibility, it's very useful for the girls to understand the process and see where they can be helpful.

- ✦ **Stage 1 Training Closing Ceremony.** Training is not complete until each girl has finished both Stages 1 & 2 and run (at least) 1 Girls' Respect Group for middle school girls. It is nice, however, to mark the end of the "all together" Stage 1 training. It's an important symbolic gesture, to thank the teens who've participated in training, honor their wisdom and effort, and welcome them to the sisterhood of Girls' Respect Groups. The specific content of the ceremony can be flexible. The heartfelt appreciation and welcome mean everything.

You can give your new Leaders a certificate. Two suggestions here: (1) You can give Leaders' certificates individually, later on, after each Leader has run her first GRG or (2) (we like this!) You can give all Leaders 2 certificates – a GRG Participant certificate at the end of Stage 1 training, and a GRG Leader certificate once they've run a GRG & completed Stage 2 training. GirlsRespectGroups.com has certificate templates for Stage 1 and Stage 2.

Individual Readiness Or When Things Aren't Working

When you're training bigger Leaders' groups, everyone may not be ready to run a GRG right after Stage 1. You'll know. Some teens may have had schedule conflicts that kept them from coming to all the training sessions. Some may need to practice their facilitation skills. Some may need more emotional maturity or focus. We keep these teens meeting with and learning from the teens who are ready and go out to lead GRGs. If they still need more support, they can attend the next training cycle. They'll have a head start! Giving out 2-stage Leaders' Training certificates allows us to recognize the participation of these girls, even if they're not quite ready to fly.

Sometimes we have to face the fact that a teen is not a good fit for GRG. Making sure that teens get **into** GRG for the right reasons is a big way to prevent surprises or disappointment later. That said, sometimes, even with the loveliest people or the best effort, it's just not right. Here are some warning signs. If a girl has any (or several) of these characteristics, she may not be a good fit at this time.

- ☑ Is she too bossy? Too talkative? Self-centered?
- ☑ Close-minded to new ideas or unable to change her own opinion?
- ☑ Doesn't let others participate?
- ☑ Does she put down others' ideas? (worse when dealing with 6th Graders!)
- ☑ Does she lose her cool easily?
- ☑ Does she show up late, miss meetings, or not participate fully? Make sure to hear her story about why she isn't showing up.
- ☑ Does she swear or present herself in a way that isn't positive for 6th Graders?
- ☑ To summarize: **Is She Respectful?**

Don't despair! There's hope for the future. With some **kind** feedback (and it's really difficult & important to be **kind** here) and some encouragement to grow, these teens can become your best Leaders of the future. When a teen comes back and shows you she's changed, it's a powerful example of effort and determination and how it can pay off! If your group is big enough and the teen is a close enough fit, find ways to keep her involved with the group in other ways, until she's ready to work with 6th Graders.

> # "Great things are not done by impulse, but by a series of small things brought together"
> *... Vincent van Gogh*

Sample Flier: GRG Leadership Training

Calling All Grade 10 Girls!
Be A Teen Leader For Girls' Respect Groups!

Teach 6th Grade Girls "What I Wish I Knew In Middle School" Make A Huge Difference In Young Girls' Lives!

A Great Volunteer Opportunity!

Respect – for ourselves and others – has a huge influence on our self-image and self-esteem. Respect drives our important life decisions – who we choose as our friends, how we approach school and work, the challenges that we accept or back away from.

Girls' Respect Groups give Grade 6 girls a chance to examine the issue of respect, understand how it can affect the rest of their lives, and learn how to make choices grounded in self-respect. Lessons learned in GRG cement a healthy foundation to help girls make good decisions through the challenging teen years.

YOU could be a teen leader, guiding girls through the difficult middle school years. Who understands *better* what middle school girls are going through?! 6th Grade girls want *so much* to talk to you, and you have important life experience to share. You can do this job better than anyone else & have a *huge* impact on these young girls!

What's in Girls' Respect Groups? This exciting 6 week program covers Respect, by Courtney Macavinta & Andrea Vander Pluym. There's time for open discussion, self-assessment quizzes, videos, games, role plays & snacks! It's a chance for emerging young women to form solid values in an encouraging and supportive environment.

You'll Lead Discussions On:

- ✪ What Respect Means To Me
- ✪ Positive & Negative Influences Of Media, Friends, & Family
- ✪ Paying Attention To Our Inner Voice
- ✪ Giving Respect & Getting It
- ✪ How To Recognize Hidden Disrespect
- ✪ How To Identify & Set Boundaries
- ✪ How To Stand Our Ground & Get Help Or Support When We Need It

Reprinted with permission
Free Spirit Publishing

How Do I Become A GRG Leader ?

GRG Leader Weekly Training Sessions This Fall
Be Ready To Run Your 1st 6 Week GRG In January!

<Teacher name> will be the <school name> advisor to the Girls' Respect Groups Leadership Program. S/he can be reached at <insert contact info>. Contact him/her to sign up!

<Lorna Blumen> is the Adult Advisor for Girls' Respect Groups and the GRG Leadership Program. <Contact Lorna at www.GirlsRespectGroups.com>. [Note: Insert your own info]

Girls' Respect Group Leadership Training Feedback Form

Leader Role

Criteria	Rating (circle one) Keep Working — Great	Strengths & Weaknesses
Completed The Lesson Plan	1 2 3 4 5	
Invited Group Participation	1 2 3 4 5	
Contributed Appropriate Personal Stories	1 2 3 4 5	
Managed Time Effectively	1 2 3 4 5	
Demonstrated Good Listening Skills	1 2 3 4 5	
Divided Work Well With Co-Leader	1 2 3 4 5	

Words To Grow By:

_____
_____
_____

Training Girls' Respect Group Leaders   45

Girls' Respect Group Leadership Training Feedback Form

Participant Role

Criteria	Rating (circle one) Keep Working — Great	Words To Grow By (My Strengths & Weaknesses)
Participation & Conduct Did I: ✓ Stay on task? ✓ Contribute positively to the discussion? ✓ Add relevant personal stories? ✓ Ask good questions? ✓ Have side conversations or go off topic?	1 2 3 4 5 1 2 3 4 5 1 2 3 4 5 1 2 3 4 5 1 2 3 4 5 1 2 3 4 5	
Responsibility Did I: ✓ Do the reading? ✓ Prepare the other homework? ✓ Review the lesson plan? ✓ Arrive on time?	1 2 3 4 5 1 2 3 4 5 1 2 3 4 5 1 2 3 4 5 1 2 3 4 5	
Overall Did I: ✓ Make a positive contribution this week? ✓ Push myself to grow this week?	1 2 3 4 5 1 2 3 4 5 1 2 3 4 5	

CHAPTER 5
How To Set Up & Run A Girls' Respect Group

Here's a step-by-step guide to setting up a Girls' Respect Group in your community. We've kept it simple, with as little time and paperwork as possible. We've even written most of the paperwork and letters for you! We're showing you how to set this up as an after school program, run at the middle school. The steps are basically the same, no matter where or when you run it. Feel free to adapt these suggestions and sample handouts for your own group. Sample handouts are also available at GirlsRespectGroups.com

Step 1: Identify Your 6th Grade Or Middle School Group & A Teacher Contact

Teacher Contact

Send an e-mail or written letter of introduction to a potential 6th Grade Teacher Contact, describing Girls' Respect Groups. See the sample letter we wrote in Sample 1. Use this letter or write your own. Invite the teacher to contact you if they'd like to run a GRG at their school, or if they have ideas or suggestions to share. Send the Girls' Respect Groups flier along with the letter. See the flier we used in Sample 2. Use it or make your own. Call or e-mail the teacher to follow up within 1 week after you send the letter.

If you're a parent wanting to set up a GRG, go talk to a teacher. Look for one of those special teachers who seems lively, energetic, humorous, kind, and curious – even at the end of the day! Ask your kids and their friends which teachers might be a good fit to be a GRG Teacher Contact. BTW, both male & female teachers are fabulous Teacher Contacts. A great teacher makes a great GRG Contact! **If you're a teacher** thinking a GRG would be cool for your school – we think you're right! Kids will love you (parents, too) for providing this opportunity for your students.

The ideal size for the group is 10 to 16 participants. You want the group to be small enough so kids get enough "air time" to talk. You want the whole group to sit around 1 table (or 4 tables pushed together) and be able to see one another. A mixed group of participants works best, not everyone from the same social group or clique.

"Misteaks r wunderfull opertunitees two lern"

... Jane Nelsen

Step 2: Identify Your Team Of High School Leaders

See the chapters on Selecting & Training GRG Leaders. If you're lucky and you've run some training sessions, you should have lots of great Leaders to choose from!

Step 3: Match Your Schedules

Identify 6 consecutive weeks, uninterrupted by vacations or holidays. Choose the same day of the week. Each session will run 90 min (really 100, with clean-up afterwards). A 4 pm start time should give enough time for the high school Leaders to reach the middle school. Allow at least 30 min after middle school ends, so the kids can have a physical break from sitting around (time for a quick run around the playground or gym).

Step 4: Specify Requirements For The Middle School

Meet with your Teacher Contact. Here are some things you'll want to talk about with the middle school Teacher Contact:

- Snack: who provides it (school or parents) & describe "healthy" (see below)
- Room
- Use Of A/V Equipment: computer, projector, TV, DVD player
- Role Of The Teacher Contact:
  - ☑ Send GRG Intro Letter home to potential participants
  - ☑ Collect & count participant registrations
  - ☑ Distribute **Respect** books to participants to prepare for Week 1
  - ☑ Make sure equipment is available, as needed, for each week
- Role of the GRG Adult Advisor: their responsibility and their discreet presence at weekly meetings. The Teacher Contact may want (or need) to be there, too.
- How to balance privacy with the need for adult supervision. How to create a safe space to encourage open conversation between high school Leaders and middle school girls, and between the girls themselves. More on privacy issues later.

- ✪ Identify the materials needed, the costs, who will supply, and who will pay – the school or the participants. The costs of running a GRG after school program can include:
    - ☑ Book
    - ☑ Handouts
    - ☑ Healthy Snack (We suggest the school provide this for weekly consistency. The school or the parents can pay)
    - ☑ High School Leaders' Fees, if paid
    - ☑ Room Rental (Most schools provide this at no charge)
    - ☑ Custodial Service (No extra charge if the custodian is still on-site)

Send home an introductory letter for potential participants and their parents, explaining the basic concept of GRG. See Sample 3.

An important note about the snack. We feel that a very important part of this program is for participants to have a healthy snack. Kids are voraciously hungry after school, and we need to give them a big and healthy snack to keep their bodies and minds working during Girls' Respect Groups. Being respectful extends to our bodies and what we put into them.

Healthy Snacks

When we say "healthy", we mean a snack with low-fat protein, complex carbohydrates, and a drink. Turkey or ham sandwiches on multi-grain bread, low-fat cheese, a vegetable or fruit platter, and water or skim milk (chocolate!!) would be a good example. Be considerate and prepared to accommodate food allergies and vegetarian options. Low-fat popcorn is another good snack. Chips and soda (that's pop to Canadians) don't cut it. It's very important to spell out clear expectations for the kind of snack, so everybody's working from the same understanding. This is especially true if there is a rotating responsibility for providing snack.

Make sure you describe the snack in the letters to the school and the participants, if parents are providing the snack. It's respectful to the Leaders that there is enough snack for them, too, especially since they're rushing from their high school to arrive at the middle school in time to run the program, often without time to stop for a snack.

> "What lies **BEHIND** us and what lies **BEFORE** us are small matters compared to what lies **WITHIN** us"
> … RW Emerson

Step 5: Purchase Respect Books

We find it's easier to purchase the books ourselves, then deliver them to the school once we know how many girls are registered for GRG. Running several or many GRGs, we can often buy books in bulk, either from a book retailer or directly from the publisher or distributor. Make some phone calls to find the best combination of price and availability. Plan for the book delivery lead time and choose your starting dates for GRG accordingly. It's best to keep a small stock of **Respect** copies on hand – enough to run one GRG (15-18 copies).

Step 6: Deliver Books To School & Send Registration Letter Home To Parents

Deliver **Respect** books to the school for all participants, early enough for participants to read Chapter 1 before the 1st meeting. Send along a registration letter to all 6th Grade participants and their parents, spelling out our expectations for their participation in GRG. The letter is to be signed by both parent & student and returned to the teacher by the 1st meeting.

Key items to cover in this registration letter: (see Sample 4)

- ✤ Date, time, & location of all meetings
- ✤ Participants commit to attend all 6 weeks
- ✤ There will be reading homework every week – 1 or 2 chapters plus a few minutes of "extra stuff" (journaling, etc)
- ✤ Must be signed by a parent & the participant
- ✤ Specify participant's costs, if any

Step 7: Collect Signed Registrations

Step 8: Organize Extra Driving Help Or Adult Advisors, If Needed

Make sure you've got enough help! If you have several GRGs running at once, you may need extra adults (parents, teachers, or older siblings) to help with driving Leaders to the middle schools. Here's where a school with the middle & high schools on the same campus have an easy time!

You will need 1 adult to stay in each classroom while the Leaders run GRG. If you're running multiple GRGs at 1 school, and the Leaders are experienced, you can have 1 adult driver/safety person who floats between GRGs.

Step 9: Prepare Materials & Handouts

Make sure every Leader has their **Respect** book and the **GRG Leadership Guide**. You will want to make a separate, complete copy of each week's Lesson Plan for

each GRG Leader. Make sure to include a copy of any reference material and the copies of the handouts for all participants. Download these files from GirlsRespectGroups.com for easy copying.

Handouts for each week are at the back of the Lesson Plan. It's easier to copy handouts for 2 or 3 weeks at a time so you don't have to keep running back to the copier. Unless you have access to a fast laser printer, it's probably faster and cheaper to take or send the handouts to a copy center for copying. Sometimes the school provides the copies, but usually it's easier (and more certain) to do it yourself. Make sure the copies are done **before** you arrive at the school. This saves crucial minutes when Leaders are rushing to get the group started on time.

Step 10: The Big Day – Week 1!!

Relax & have fun! The next 7 chapters are all about the nuts & bolts of running the weekly Girls' Respect Group meetings. We've got you covered! Read on!

Sample 1: Intro Letter To Teachers (Or Parents)

Letter Of Introduction To Teachers

Dear <Teacher>,

<Maria Lopez> mentioned that you were interested in the **Girls' Respect Groups** after school program. I've enclosed some info for you. If you'd like to run a group in your school this fall or winter, please let me know. If you have any ideas or suggestions, we'd love to hear them!

Girls' Respect Groups 6 Week After School Program

Our 6 week GRG program for 6th Grade girls is based on the book **Respect**, by Courtney Macavinta and Andrea Vander Pluym. Our motivation: We want to help 6th Grade girls anchor their sense of self-respect, respect for others, and their ability to ask for respect. Support at this critical stage can prevent or minimize many middle & high school level problems. While supporting girls in 6th Grade is ideal, it's never too late and those same ideas apply equally to women (& men) of any age.

Reprinted with permission
Free Spirit Publishing

Girls' Respect Groups are unique. After school sessions are led by specially selected & trained high school teen girls, acting as mentors and leaders to the younger girls. Sharing their experience and stories, teen leaders extend a steadying hand to the younger girls, guiding them through the rough spots. An added benefit: The teen leaders re-examine their own ideas about respect, while learning valuable leadership and facilitation skills. Leaders get Community Service credit for hours worked. Teen leaders work under the supervision of a GRG Adult Advisor.

The program costs include: a book & curriculum materials for each participant (approx $30 per participant), and the cost of a healthy snack, provided each week by the school. [Note: If your group Leaders or Adult Advisor will be paid, identify the costs here]

I've attached the following information:

- Flier for the Girls' Respect Groups program
- Letter to be sent home to parents & possible participants explaining the program
- Comments from a school group of 6th Grade girls who participated
- Recommendation Letter from a 6th Grade Teacher Contact

<Insert your relevant work or community experience, & past experience running GRG groups.>

I'll call you next week to touch base.

Regards,

<Your name>
Girls' Respect Groups Adult Advisor <plus relevant work title>
<Your contact info>

Sample 2: Flier For GRG

Flier For Girls' Respect Groups

6th Grade Girls' Respect Groups

- ☑ What's Respect?
- ☑ How To Get It? Give It?
- ☑ How Does Media Shape My Opinions?
  - ☆ Of Myself?
  - ☆ My Friends?
- ☑ Get The Straight Scoop From High School Girls Who've Lived It!
- ☑ How Can I Tell Who My Real Friends Are?
- ☑ How & When To Stand Up For Myself?
- ☑ Why Is Gossip So Bad?

- ☑ 6 Weeks, 6 Meetings!
- ☑ After School 4:00 - 5:40 pm
- ☑ Readings From Respect & respectrx.com
- ☑ Small Group Discussions
  - ☆ Express Yourself!
  - ☆ Have Fun!
  - ☆ Great Info From Videos & Games!
- ☑ Groups Led By Local High School Teen Girls Selected & Trained In Leadership & Facilitation
- ☑ Start A Group In Your Community!

Join Us!!

Interested? Contact: <MarySmith@xyz.com>

Respect cover reprinted with permission Free Spirit Publishing

How To Set Up & Run A Girls' Respect Group

Sample 3: *Letter For 6th Grade Girls & Parents*

6th Grade Girls' Respect Group

6 Wednesdays After School: Starting Oct 3, 4:00 - 5:40 pm
Sign Up Now!

Respect – for ourselves and others – is a crucial cornerstone of self-image and self-esteem. Respect drives our important life decisions – who we choose as our friends, how we approach school and work, the challenges that we accept or back away from. The preteen years are so important, to develop and cement a healthy foundation that will prepare girls to make good decisions through their challenging teen years.

Girls' Respect Groups give Grade 6 girls a chance to examine the issue of respect, understand how it can affect the rest of their lives, and learn how to make choices that are grounded in self-respect. Excitingly, this group will be led by 2 female high school students. Who understands better what middle school girls are going through?

The 6 Week GRG Program Covers:

- What Respect Means To Me
- Positive & Negative Influences Of Media, Friends, & Family
- Paying Attention To Our Inner Voice
- Giving Respect & Getting It
- How To Recognize Hidden Disrespect
- How To Identify & Set Boundaries
- How To Stand Our Ground & Get Help When We Need It

Reprinted with permission
Free Spirit Publishing

It's a wonderful opportunity for preteens to work closely with great young women who generously share their experience and insights with the next generation of girls (What I Wish I Knew In 6th Or 7th Grade!). Each week covers a new topic and a new chapter from the recent book **Respect** by Courtney Macavinta and Andrea Vander Pluym. There's time for open discussion and a chance for our emerging young women to form solid values in an encouraging and supportive environment.

<Lorna Blumen> is the Adult Advisor for this Girls' Respect Group and will attend GRG meetings. Lorna is an educational consultant in Toronto, Canada. She runs workshops on Bullying Prevention for Elementary & Middle School, Conflict Resolution Skills, & Stress Survival Strategies. Lorna was on Parent Education Network's Board of Directors from 1997-2006. She has appeared on local & national TV and radio, at international conferences, and has contributed to articles in national magazines for parents & teachers. Lorna can be reached at **GirlsRespectGroups.com**. <Replace with your own info>

<6th Grade Teacher> will be the <school> Teacher Contact and will attend GRG meetings.

This Is A Great Opportunity For Every Grade 6 Female!
ONLY 15 Spaces — Sign Up Now!!
Contact Your Teacher For Registration Info!

Sample 4: 6th Grade GRG Registration Form

Welcome To 6th Grade Girls' Respect Group!
6 Wednesdays After School: Starting Oct 3, 4:00 - 5:40 pm
<Arthur Franklin Middle School>

Before our 1st meeting, please get a copy of **Respect** by Courtney Macavinta & Andrea Vander Pluym from your teacher, <insert teacher's name>. **Please read the Intro & Chapter 1** (What Respect Means To You) for our 1st meeting. Chapter 1 is the most important chapter in the book. It explains what we mean by respect, so please make sure you read it & come prepared to share your knowledge!

We want to be clear about our expectations for your participation in GRG:

1. We expect you to come to all 6 meetings
2. A (big, healthy) snack will be served at each meeting
3. Every week we'll focus on a new topic. You'll have 1 or (rarely) 2 chapters to read. GRG is much better if everyone does their homework
4. There may be extra activities for you to do at home – keep a journal (no more than 5 min a day, unless you want to do more), collect magazine examples or pictures, or pay attention when you watch TV and take notes
5. We want you to feel comfortable to talk & share your thoughts, experiences & feelings
6. You'll get out of this what you put into it. Our GRG Leaders, 2 high school girls, come prepared to lead the meetings. Like you, they're really busy with homework & activities. We expect you to make time in your busy schedules to do your part of the work, too
7. We really appreciate your help with room set up and clean up. The high school Leaders are rushing to get to you, so having the room & snacks ready means an on-time start!
8. Parent pick up is 5:40pm, allowing 10 min for everyone to clean up & collect coats & backpacks. Weeks 1 & 6 will end at 5:50pm.
9. The school should have contacted you about the program cost <insert costs and arrangements for payment>
10. Please return this letter, signed by the participant & a parent, to your teacher by the 1st meeting. Keep a copy for yourself.

Please contact the Girls' Respect Group Adult Advisor, <insert Advisor's name>, with questions or ideas at <insert Advisor's contact info>.

Can't wait to meet you! See you in a few weeks!

_____
Parent Signature

_____ _____
Participant Signature   Parent Name - Print

_____ _____
Participant Name - Print   Parent Contact - Telephone & e-mail

CHAPTER 6
6 Weekly Lesson Plans: Tips For Every Week

Now we're ready to jump right to the heart of this program – the 6 weeks of the GRG after school program. Every week has its own topic, and the next 6 chapters go week-by-week to give you a full, 90 min program to run for an eager group of 6th Grade girls. Before we get down to the weekly nitty-gritty, here are some helpful tips that apply to every week.

In each week's Lesson Plan you will find:

- ✡ **Reference Material List**. Identifies the **Respect** chapter that you'll cover this week.

- ✡ **Class Materials List.** All materials that Leaders will need to bring or have available for this week's meeting are listed at the beginning of each week's plan. The Class Materials list quickly tells you how to prepare for and what to bring with you to GRG. The list covers everything you will need for that week, from computers and audio/visual materials you should ask the school to make available, to pencils and markers for every participant. You must figure out which materials need to be supplied by the school, which by Leaders, and to coordinate who's responsible for each item so they all arrive.

- ✡ **Some Materials Listed In Week 1 Need To Be Supplied Every Week** – the room, table(s) with enough chairs, snack, pens & pencils, etc. You may need to be clear with the school that you'd like the same room every week. **Ask for a room that won't have people coming and going while you're meeting**. A healthy snack needs to be provided every week, too, by the school or parents, and that can take some planning.

- ✡ **Your Meeting Room Will Require Some Setup** – rearranging of desks, tables, and chairs. The middle school girls and their teacher can be asked to do this before the Leaders arrive. Leaders are always in a rush to get from their school to the middle school, and this will help make sure the group starts on time.

- ✡ **Clean Up**. Be clear with the girls that it's everybody's job to clean up the room and return it to its original condition – tables & chairs moved back, snacks cleaned up. Often, you're using another teacher's room. Be good citizens and thank the teacher & the students for sharing their room, desks, and materials. Make sure parents waiting in the halls know that the girls will be cleaning up.

- ✡ **A/V Equipment.** For weeks when you're showing videos, **make sure you have access to a TV & DVD player or a computer with a multimedia projector** (if the group is small enough, you may not need the projector). It's a good idea to **call or e-mail your Teacher Contact 1 or 2 days before, just to remind them of this week's A/V needs** and to have the equipment available in the meeting room (or make the computer lab available, for example).

- ✡ **Bring Name Tags For The Leaders & Girls.** For the first few weeks, it'll help the Leaders learn everyone's name. Some of the girls may not know each other, especially if GRG is at the start of the school year, or if 6th Grade is a new school for some or all. Also, it's nice for the Adult Advisor to greet and introduce yourself to parents the 1st day.

- ✡ **Handouts.** The handouts for each week are listed in the Class Materials section at the top of each Lesson Plan and *again* under the Activity Number where you'll actually use it. When you see the handout name again at the beginning of Activity 6, for example, you'll know to pull it out now!

- ✡ **Handouts Are At The Back Of Each Lesson Plan**. Be sure to make enough copies for all participants. **Yes, you have our permission to copy the Lesson Plans and Handouts**. Download copies at **GirlsRespectGroups.com.** If you develop some great activities and handouts, send them in and we'll pass them along to other GRG Leaders!

- ✡ **Folders & Journals For The Girls**. In addition to the **Respect** book, which the girls should have picked up well before the 1st meeting (don't forget to make arrangements to drop off the books, so participants can do their reading), we always give each participant her own journal and a 2-pocket folder at Week 1. Ask everyone to be sure to bring these, along with the book, every week. The dollar store is a great source for these materials!

- ✡ **Homework**. Last week's and next week's homework are listed on each lesson plan. When girls have homework, it's really nice if Leaders go that extra mile to do the homework, too. For example, in Week 2, we give the girls journals and ask them to journal for 5 min every day for the next week. We really recommend that the Leaders journal at least 2-3 days that week, too. The Leaders' authenticity of "walking your talk" means a lot to the 6th Grade girls.

- ✡ **Icebreakers**. There's an icebreaker to begin every week except the last. Feel free to use your own and let us know if the icebreakers you use (yours or ours) are especially good at team building and friend-making. Icebreakers are also a good physical and mental change of pace. Sometimes it's nice to do a 2nd, short icebreaker or do some quick role plays after 60 min to have a break from sitting.

- ✬ **Time Estimates For Each Activity**. Activity times will vary every time you run a group, depending on the girls who are participating and what's going on in their lives at that exact moment. Don't worry – the group will run the way it's supposed to run. If there's a real "hot issue" going on, it's respectful to make the extra time to talk about it and work it through. It's ok if you don't get to all the activities, but you do want to keep an eye out for time. We'll talk more about this in the section on "How To Move Ahead".

    Watch The Time Discreetly. Put a watch on the table in front of you. As part of your preparation, pencil in the clock time next to each activity on your lesson plan, so you can see if you're running on time. In other words, if the group runs from 4-5:40 pm, during Week 1, Activity 1 will start at 4 pm, Activity 2 at 4:20 pm, Activity 3 at 4:30 pm, etc.

- ✬ **Week 1 Is The Most Hectic Week, So Give Yourselves 10 Extra Min, 100 Total.** Lots of introductions & setting up the ground rules, in addition to covering a very important chapter in the book, Chapter 1, "What Respect Means To You". **Week 6 is longer too, also scheduled for 100 min**. It contains wrap up exercises and saying goodbye, which takes a while for girls who've grown close over 6 weeks. Please advise parents so they can adjust pick up times.

    You Can Achieve Anything You Put Your Mind To

- ✬ **Using The Respect Book**. Many activities refer to **Respect**. If so, we list the book and the page number next to the activity title, for the Leaders' use. Sometimes, it's best for the girls to follow along in the book. If so, we suggest "open to **Respect**, p 45", for example.

- ✬ **Help Us Improve! Surveys For Every Week**. You'll want to know what parts of the program mean the most to the girls, and which parts don't work so well for your group. Make sure you leave time at the end of every meeting for girls to fill out the surveys and leave them with you. They're useful for your planning, as you customize GRG for your own groups, and we'd like to hear from you, too. Feel free to send us a copy of these feedback forms. There's a wrap up survey in Week 6 that asks for suggestions about the overall program.

- ✬ **Girls' Respect Group Garden Handout**. At the back of Week 1, there's a handout with 2 flowers with petals big enough to write in. At the end of every week, ask the girls to fill in 2 petals with 2 ideas or things they learned or discussed that they really liked and want to remember from this week's meeting (1 idea per petal). At the end of the 6 weeks, each girl will have a beautiful "garden" of 12 ideas she'd like to carry forward from GRG. The girls may like to share their garden ideas with each other. It makes a great icebreaker for the beginning of the next week.

Here are a few generally useful tips:

- ✩ **Every Leader Should Have & Bring Her Own Copy Of The Week's Lesson Plan.** You could use the lesson plans directly in this book, but it's more flexible to make a copy of each week's lesson plan every time you run a GRG. Then you can make notes, enter the name of the chosen Leader in front of each activity, make changes, & pencil in clock times of each activity. We don't give participants the lesson plans, just the handouts. Too much paper!

- ✩ **Review Your Lesson Plan 3-4 Days Ahead & Identify Materials To Print, Copy, Or Hand Out.** Most of the handouts are at the back of each lesson plan, and some weeks you'll need to look up some Internet info. When you get to the meeting room, put the handouts in easy reach for later

- ✩ **Friends.** Even though Friends is the topic for Week 5, **the issue of friends will come up EVERY week** – it's huge at this age & stage. Be prepared to weave some friends' issues into the conversation, yet find a balance so Friends isn't the *only* topic every week! It's fine to suggest, "OK, 2 more ideas, then let's bring this up again when we get to Friends week." Make a note and be sure to raise it again when you get there. **Honestly, every week will be a leadership job to balance "hot issues" – the need to talk now AND not getting pulled too far off topic.**

- ✩ **Use Current Examples.** Some of your GRG discussions will be about TV shows, celebrities, or ads that are popular right now, but trends & favorites change quickly, so make sure to stay up to date. For example, in Week 3, Media Influence, you'll talk about Celebrities Without Makeup (they look just like us!) and Celebrity Clothing Choices (how your clothes speak for you). Instead of giving you pictures of celebs that are so yesterday, we point you to websites where you can find pictures of today's style makers.

    You can also search the Internet for pictures of "celebrities without makeup" or "celebrity clothing" or look at pictures from recent acting or music awards show. If you have a computer in your GRG room, you can view them online, or you can print a copy to bring to GRG to show some examples. Give the girls website info so they can search for other examples. You could also assign this as homework to look up before Week 3.

- **Use Of Online Video & Print Materials.** There are weeks where we refer you to short clips from movies or videos to view online, bring in from home, or purchase a copy. For example, in Media Week, we point you to an awesome video on the Dove website created for the Campaign For Real Beauty. It shows how they computer edit pictures of a teen model to make her look (unattainably) "better" (OMG – they even make her neck longer and skinnier by computer!). Even as we speak, more videos are coming out on that website that support girls' and women's natural beauty and encourage us to use our own brains and hearts to decide what looks good on us.

- **Be Aware Of Copyright Restrictions**. You're welcome to copy all the lesson plans and handouts we created for this book, to use when you're running GRGs. We think it's important to make it easy to share this material. There are other materials in the lesson plan that we loved but we didn't create (like the **Respect** book). We asked the creators & received permission to use or refer to some of these materials in our book. You'll see a reference at the bottom of the page. Please use these materials in keeping with the Educational & Fair Use Guidelines of the Copyright Act.

- **Pick Up Times.** The sessions run 90 min long & they're packed! Please allow 10 additional min for cleaning up snack materials, moving tables and chairs, and collecting materials to go home. We suggest that you ask parents to pick kids up after 1 hour, 40 min (100 min). Remember that Weeks 1 & 6 are 100 min long; ask parents for a 1 hour, 50 min pick up on those days.

- ✡ **Make Sure To Ask The Participants For Their Help Cleaning Up**, and thank them for their help setting up. Leaders are usually rushing from school, so the girls' set up means an on-time start!

- ✡ **Plan Weekly Meetings Of Co-Leaders & Adult Advisor(s) During GRG** to review the pluses and minuses of each week. It's great to go out for dinner or a quick snack right after each GRG meeting while ideas are still fresh.

- ✡ **Adult Advisor(s)**. Please remember, a GRG Adult Advisor should (and probably must) be present at all GRG meetings, for safety. That said, your role is in the background, not at the table. Find a place in the room where you can sit unobtrusively, so your presence does not interfere too much with open conversation. It's helpful for you to have your own copy of the week's lesson plan, so you can time sections and take notes on how to customize or improve. This will be very useful at your weekly meetings with Leaders.

We're not sure how to say this nicely, but ... **Adult Advisors should rarely speak during GRG meetings**. Even if things run a little long or get a little noisy, your teen Leaders will grow most as Leaders if you let them sort out the rough spots. You can have a helpful, discreet hand signal to mean "think you should move on", but the Leaders need practice and the 6th Grade girls need to know that it's the Leaders, not you, running the group. Of course, please be friendly and feel free to chat when you're setting up and cleaning up the room, or handing out supplies, and you'll want to help the Leaders & turn the DVD player on, for example, to keep things flowing (Note: Set up any A/V equipment before you begin the group & cue any videos to their starting point). The one thing that **does** need an Adult Advisor's intervention is when a Big Problem is revealed – threats of impending harm, fear of suicide, abuse, guns, etc. This could need the Teacher Contact's help, too, and maybe the police. Read more about Big Problems in our **Handle This!** chapter later.

Special Note #1: As a Leader, always remember to be respectful of the 6th Graders. Some 6th Graders have way more knowledge and life experience than you'd expect, sometimes more than you, even if it can be incomplete. The problems they are facing, especially with friends, sometimes with family, can be heart breaking and seem insurmountable to them. A respectful, sympathetic ear and a shoulder to lean on can help a kid find her own inner strength. You are *not* expected to have all the answers or know how to solve serious life problems. You *are* expected to treat all the people you meet and work with respectfully and with dignity.

Special Note #2: These lesson plans, notes, and suggestions are given to you with the hope that you'll use them to run the most amazing GRG ever! That said, **they are NOT for you to memorize or read aloud word-for-word**. You must spend enough time in your training and weekly preparation to run a group, including reading **Respect**, reading your Lesson Plans, and talking with your Co-Leader, that you feel comfortable with the material and concepts.

Don't stray too far from the lesson plan – the school (or organizer) is expecting you to deliver this specific curriculum. If you have great ideas for extra topics or you've developed a lesson plan on your own, extend your GRG for an extra week or 2. If you want our help turning your ideas into a lesson plan or want to share your newly-created lesson plan with the GRG Leaders' Network, share it on GirlsRespectGroups.com!

Also, remember that GRG is a discussion group for the girls, so make sure there's enough time and space for the girls to talk – to you and each other. Spice it up!

References to & reprints from *Respect: A Girl's Guide to Getting Respect & Dealing When Your Line is Crossed*, Courtney Macavinta & Andrea Vander Pluym, ©2005, with permission Free Spirit Press

CHAPTER 7
GRG WEEK 1
What Respect Means To Me

Reference Material: Respect, Courtney Macavinta & Andrea Vander Pluym, Intro & Chapter 1

Class Materials:

- Large open table(s), big enough to hold everyone, their books, & snacks
- Snack (school provides)
- Respect book for each participant (distributed earlier)
- Journal/Notebook for each participant (spiral bound, 5x7 or bigger, 50-100 pgs)
- 2-pocket folder for each participant
- Pencil/Pen for each participant (school or participant provides)
- **Handouts**
  - Getting To Know You Interviews
  - What Does Respect Mean To You?
  - Help Us Improve! Week 1
  - GRG Garden
  - GRG Online Resources
  - GRG Assignments
- Chart paper & Markers (4 boxes)
- Name tags

Last Week's Homework: Read Respect, Intro & Chapter 1
Leaders: Prepare a few personal stories to illustrate the Respect Basics

Run Time
100 min

"Never settle for anything less than your best"
... *Brian Tracy*

GRG WEEK 1
What Respect Means To Me

Activity 1: Introductions & Icebreaker   **20/20 min**

Handout: Getting To Know You

- ✬ **Introduce Leaders:**
    - ✓ Who you are, how you got involved, share 1-2 fun facts about you

- ✬ **Icebreaker: Getting To Know You (GTKY Handout)**
    - ✓ Break into 2s & interview each other
    - ✓ Leaders: time for 3 min; then switch
    - ✓ Return to group & share 1 min intros of each other (Leaders: Time 1 min each)

Activity 2: Purpose & Goals Of Girls' Respect Groups (Respect, Intro)   **10/30 min**

Note: Explain there's a lot of "set-up" today & usually there will be more relaxed talking

- ✬ Based on the book **Respect** by Courtney Macavinta & Andrea Vander Pluym
    - ✓ Adults looking back don't understand their lack of confidence in middle/high school
    - ✓ Realize the problems it caused them & the bad decisions they sometimes made
    - ✓ We look back from high school & feel the same way
    - ✓ Now realize it was caused by lack of respect – for ourselves & others
    - ✓ **Give you some shortcuts to some hard lessons**
    - ✓ **Help you choose friends to rely on & help each other** (already doing this)

GRG WEEK 1
What Respect Means To Me

Activity 2: Purpose & Goals Of Girls' Respect Groups (continued...)   **10/30 min**

- ✪ **Goals For This Group:**

    - ✓ **What is respect**? How do you give it and get it? For yourself & others
    - ✓ Understand **why respect is so important**
    - ✓ How **respect** (or lack) **influences your choices & decisions**
    - ✓ Help you **choose friends & build friendships based on respect**
    - ✓ Influence **choices now & later** – schools, school groups, romances, work situations
    - ✓ Handle **family & relatives**, teachers, other adults (most difficult to handle with respect)
    - ✓ Influence of **media** (ads focus on being impossibly thin; buy this & you'll have BF/GF)
    - ✓ **Society's expectations** – "be smart & independent, but package yourself as hot"
    - ✓ **How to balance**
    - ✓ **Bad situations & relationships** – how to fix or leave
    - ✓ Big Picture: **This is really "figuring out who you are & what you stand for"**
        - ▪ Not a simple quiz; takes time & thinking & testing
        - ▪ Helps to have support from your friends

- ✪ **Why Do We Need & Want Respect?** (ask group)

- ✪ When people respect themselves & receive respect:

    - ✓ More confident
    - ✓ More willing to try & learn new things; Stretch & grow
    - ✓ Considerate of others
    - ✓ Happy being themselves
    - ✓ Know their rights & know they deserve respect
    - ✓ Know how to (respectfully) stand up for themselves

GRG WEEK 1
What Respect Means To Me

Activity 3: GRG Privacy & Respect Guidelines   5/35 min

✯ For this group to really work, we must create a **welcoming, safe space where we're all encouraged to try new ideas & activities, to share, to grow**

- ✓ Everything shared stays in the room – respect each other's privacy
- ✓ No putting others down, even when you disagree
- ✓ Respect everyone
- ✓ Let others finish speaking before interrupting
- ✓ Encouraged to disagree – respectfully!
- ✓ Consider other viewpoints & sometimes change your thinking
- ✓ Encouraged to share – don't have to
- ✓ Ask: *Other ideas?*
- ✓ Encouraged to tell stories – be sure to do it kindly
- ✓ No names even (or especially) if everybody knows the people in story
- ✓ Ideas for respectful ways to ask for quiet or time to move on?
    - T for time
    - Peace sign
- ✓ Ask: *Other suggestions?*

✯ Keep In Mind:

- ✓ **Respect applies to everyone, not just you ... parents, teens, children, etc**
- ✓ Slightly adjust all info to fit you (be flexible & pick what works)
- ✓ Some situations apply now; some will apply later
- ✓ You will get out of GRG what you put into it
- ✓ You're the expert on you and know yourself best

RESPONSIBILITY

GRG WEEK 1
What Respect Means To Me

Activity 3: GRG Privacy & Respect Guidelines (continued...) **5/35 min**

✭ Our Responsibility To Keep You Safe

- ✓ We want everyone to be safe

- ✓ Similar to teachers' responsibility

- ✓ If we hear something that will hurt you or someone else, we (legally) have to tell an adult (suicidal, plans to hurt someone else, sexual abuse)

- ✓ **Note to Leaders**: Best practices from police and Children's Aid on how to handle this are changing, but are not universal. New thinking suggests you **shouldn't** say that you have to tell an adult, because it shuts down communication from a child who is in trouble & needs help. **A child who tells you about a big problem does so because he or she needs your help NOW, disclaimers or no!** Adult Advisors & Leaders should discuss how to set the right tone for care & protection of participants and how to handle disclosures of a big problem

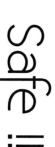

Be Safe!

Activity 4: What Is Respect? **5/40 min**
Handout: What Does Respect Mean To You?

✭ **Respect** defined as: to give regard, honor, & consideration

✭ Easier to describe it or see the difference between respect & disrespect

✭ **Respect Is:**   **Respect Isn't:**

- ♥ Feeling good about yourself   💣 Being filled with self doubt
- ♥ Being listened to   💣 Being ignored
- ♥ Doing what you want with your life   💣 Doing what someone else decides for you
- ♥ A conversation   💣 A screaming match
- ♥ "No means No"   💣 "No means Yes"

Other examples? (Fill in handout)

GRG WEEK 1
What Respect Means To Me

Activity 5: 7 Respect Basics (open to Respect, p 6) **30/70 min**

✩ Go around the room, everyone pick a "Basic"; explain it & tell why you feel it's important

✩ Leaders fill in extra ideas OR

✩ Go around the room with each Basic (depends on group size)

✩ Leaders: Remember to offer a few of your own stories

✩ **Remember to ask *"What Do You Think?"***

1. **Having Self-Respect (3 min)**

    ✓ Self-Respect – respecting yourself as a human being

    ✓ You're fine just the way you are (we all want to grow & improve)

    ✓ **Respect starts on the inside**

    ✓ **If you don't treat yourself with respect, nobody else will**

    ✓ Listen to your feelings, figure out what you believe in, make good choices for you

    ✓ Important to take time to think it through

    ✓ With practice, it becomes easier to decide quickly & to stand up for yourself

    ✓ Learn from mistakes without putting yourself down

2. **Listening To Your Gut (4 min)**

    ✓ Body & mind signals; deep down sense

    ✓ Ever happened to you?

    - Followed by or in elevator with someone creepy?
    - Did you get out? Go the other way?
    - Has anyone asked you to do something wrong?
    - What did you do?

    ✓ **Key: If you keep silencing your gut feeling, eventually you lose touch with it**

GRG WEEK 1
What Respect Means To Me

Activity 5: 7 Respect Basics (continued...)   **30/70 min**

- ✓ **Why & when do you not listen to your gut?**
    - Embarrassed or afraid to look bad
    - Please others
    - Not let others down
    - Easier to do what's more popular or accepted
    - Ask: *Other ideas?*

3. **Setting Boundaries (2 min)**

    - ✓ **Boundary** – a line you set that you don't want others to cross
    - ✓ Boundaries: How someone...
        - Speaks to you
        - Treats you
        - Touches you
    - ✓ Everyone's boundaries are a little different
    - ✓ Related to your personal limits, values, life experiences
    - ✓ **How to know when your boundary has been crossed?**
    - ✓ Feel uncomfortable
    - ✓ How to tell people they've crossed your boundary?
        - *"I don't feel comfortable when you _____"*
        - *"Please don't do that around me anymore"* (find your own words)
    - ✓ Easier to set it up for success
        - *"I need to go home right after the movie"*
        - *"Let's not talk about her if she's not here"*
        - Say it **before** the wrong thing happens or it's hard to find the words to fix it

GRG Week 1   73

GRG WEEK 1
What Respect Means To Me

Activity 5: 7 Respect Basics (continued...) **30/70 min**

- ✓ How to express good boundary experiences? (not always complaining)
  - *"Thanks for respecting my boundaries"* (listening to me, not pushing me)
  - *"Thanks"* (non-specific); Smile (non-verbal ways to say thanks)
  - *"Let's get together again"*
  - Find your own words; Reinforce when someone treats you the right way

4. **Speaking Up (2 min)**
   - ✓ **We deserve to be heard; Shows self-respect**
   - ✓ **Why don't we speak up?**

   - Afraid of being judged
   - Afraid we don't have anything worthwhile to say
   - Feel shy at 1st
   - Out of touch with self – Don't know what you want to say
   - ✓ Takes courage to be honest about feelings, opinions, boundaries, *especially* when you disagree with friends or family or adults
   - ✓ Speaking your mind easier for some people (based on personality, experience)
   - ✓ **Practice:** Learn how to speak without crushing someone else
     - OK to disagree, but show respect for others
   - ✓ **Benefit:** When you're clear, people learn how to treat you (takes time)

SET YOUR BOUNDARIES
& SPEAK YOUR MIND

GRG WEEK 1
What Respect Means To Me

Activity 5: 7 Respect Basics (continued...) **30/70 min**

5. Building Strong Relationships (3 min)

- ✓ **Get respect by giving it 1st – especially to other girls**
- ✓ **Get to know people before judging them**
- ✓ Respect people for **who they are inside**, *not* their clothes, what they have, their looks
- ✓ Easy to blow someone off; takes time to look inside
- ✓ If you look inside others, people will be willing to look inside you

6. Fighting For Equality (3 min)

- ✓ Equality not just for girls
- ✓ All human beings, backgrounds, ways of life deserve equal treatment
- ✓ **Stand up for your rights & rights of others**
- ✓ Big Issues (world peace) & Small Issues (respect boys & ask for respect from boys)
- ✓ Speak out against injustice – don't be a bystander
- ✓ Organize others to take a stand
- ✓ World still not equal, but believe you are equal, despite any discrimination

7. Getting Help (3 min)

- ✓ Sometimes know you're not getting respect, but don't know how to stop it
- ✓ Hard to admit you can't do it alone, need help
- ✓ Takes time to make changes
- ✓ Takes time to open people's eyes to your need for respect, your changes

GRG WEEK 1
What Respect Means To Me

Activity 5: 7 Respect Basics (continued...)   **30/70 min**

---

7. Getting Help (3 min) (continued...)

- ✓ Hard to stand up to adults (parents, teachers, employers, coaches) & get results without going too far (yelling, swearing, slamming doors, quitting)
- ✓ Can help to get another adult on your side; Friend to talk to
- ✓ Online info sources (handout later)

Activity 6: Disrespect (Respect, p 11)   **10/80 min**

- ✯ Ask: *Define disrespect?*
- ✯ **Disrespect**: When someone violates any of your rights
- ✯ **Disrespect, esp. when it continues, makes it hard to keep your own self-respect**
- ✯ **Easy to see in others, hard to look at myself & notice I'm being disrespectful**
- ✯ Might not look like it, but people who disrespect others usually have little self-respect
- ✯ Joking ok up to a point; Watch for **"Ouch Point"**
- ✯ People disrespect each other in many ways
- ✯ **Common forms of disrespect:**

    - ✓ **Using Fear & Intimidation**
        - ⇨ Using pressure or power over someone to gain respect
        - ⇨ Ex: Bullies on the playground
        - ⇨ Ex: Threats from adults
        - ⇨ Ex: Threats to ruin your reputation; Threats to not be your friend

    - ✓ **Acting "Above" Others**
        - ⇨ People try to act better than others, think others will respect & envy them
        - ⇨ Ex: Groups of girlfriends that don't "allow" others in
        - ⇨ Ex: You answer a question in class & classmates laugh at what you're saying
        - ⇨ Ex: When you don't respect others' opinions, *especially* when you disagree
        - ⇨ **Respect ≠ Agree**

GRG WEEK 1
What Respect Means To Me

Activity 6: Disrespect (continued...)   **10/80 min**

✓ **Ordering People Around**

- People try to pressure you: ideas or actions
- Think you respect them if they can make you do stuff; not true
- Ex: Have to do/think/wear the same as your group of friends
- Pushing people around against their will is disrespectful
- People with more power **will** ask you to do things – Teacher, Boss, Parent, Adult
- **Depends on what they ask and how they ask**
- They can require us to do stuff, but still should treat us respectfully
- More likely you would do it if they ask politely
- May not want to do housework, **but** parents have a right to expect our help as long as they're not screaming at us
- Teachers can set a due date for a paper, but they shouldn't call us morons
- Employers can ask us to work late, but they shouldn't swear at us

"Learn to love & approve of yourself. This is the first step to achieving greater things"
... Vanessa Lampert

GRG WEEK 1
What Respect Means To Me

Activity 7: Fill In Help Us Improve! & GRG Garden 10/90 min

Handouts: Help Us Improve!, GRG Garden, Online Resources, GRG Assignments

For Next Week:

- ✓ Review GRG Assignments handout
- ✓ **Bring your book, folder, journal, pen, & GRG Garden handout EVERY WEEK**
- ✓ Read Chapters 2 & 3, Your Mind & Your Body
- ✓ Bring in a teen magazine

Note: We've allowed 10 extra minutes for this 1st week, which often runs long, for a total of 100 min

GRG WEEK 1
Getting To Know You

Directions: Please interview your partner   **Time:** 3 min each

- Describe yourself in 2 sentences

- Describe your family. Do you have pets?

- What's your astrological sign? (ex. Leo, Aries)

- What schools have you been to?

- What are your interests at school? Favorite subjects?

- After school & out of school activities?

- What's your favorite food?

- What's the last movie you saw? Did you like it?

GRG WEEK 1
What Does Respect Mean To You?

Respect Is:
- Feeling good about yourself
- Being listened to
- Doing what you want with your life
- A conversation
- "No means No"

Respect Isn't:
- Being filled with self doubt
- Being ignored
- Doing what someone else decides
- A screaming match
- "No means Yes"

Respect	Disrespect
♥	💣
♥	💣
♥	💣
♥	💣
♥	💣

Define Respect in 1 sentence:

80 Girls' Respect Groups

Help Us Improve!!

GRG WEEK 1

What Respect Means To Me

What 3 Ideas Or Activities Did You Like Best This Week?

1.

2.

3.

Anything We Should Cut? Or Improve?

1.

2.

3.

Other Comments? Your Ideas Help Us A Lot!! Thanks!

Girls' Respect Groups Idea Garden

Name:_____

Every week, write your 2 favorite ideas in a petal. After 6 weeks, every petal will have an idea inside it for you to remember!

GRG WEEK 1
Girls' Respect Groups Online Resources

**Note: Most sites have great info for everyone – students, teachers & parents
Check 'em all out!**

Inspirational Websites For Girls:

- girlsrespectgroups.com
- respectrx.com
- gcdamagazine.com
- smartgirl.org
- deebest.com
- hardygirlshealthywomen.org
- girleffect.org
- campaignforrealbeauty.com
- media-awareness.ca

Bullying Prevention Websites:

- bullying.org
- cyberbullying.ca
- cyberbully.org
- stopbullyingnow.hrsa.gov
- safety-council.org/info/child/bullies.html
- nfb.ca (look up It's A Girl's World movie)
- canadiansafeschools.com
- teamheroes.ca
- antibullying.net
- bullying.co.uk
- prevnet.ca
- breakthecycle.org
- safeschoolsforall.com
- stopbullyingworld.org
- cyberbullyinghelp.com
- stopbullyingnow.com

**Note: These websites were verified at publication, but the Internet changes quickly.
If you find changes, please tell us, & we'll pass it on.
Let us know about good resources that you discover, too!**

GRG WEEK 1
GRG Assignments

Bring Respect, Journal, Folder, Pen & GRG Garden Handout Every Week!!

For Week 1:
✧ Read Respect, Intro & Chapter 1, What Respect Means To You

For Week 2:
✧ Read Respect, Chapters 2 & 3, Your Mind & Your Body

✧ Bring in a teen magazine

For Week 3:
✧ Read Respect, Chapter 4, Your Media IQ

✧ Keep A Journal! activity

✧ 1 week log of all positive & negative self-talk

✧ Bring in a teen magazine

✧ Think of or find a picture of 1 positive role model & 1 negative role model

✧ For each picture, write down why you think they're a role model

  ✓ 1-2 things you admire about them
  ✓ 1-2 things you don't admire about them

For Week 4:
✧ Read Respect, Chapter 5, Family

✧ Look up media websites

For Week 5:
✧ Read Respect, Chapters 6 & 11, Friends & Fighting For Your Rights At School

For Week 6:
✧ Read Respect, Chapter 7, Relationships

CHAPTER 8
GRG WEEK 2
Your Mind & Your Body

Reference Material: Respect, Chapters 2 & 3

Class Materials:

- ✯ Pictures Of Stars Without Makeup & Celebrities' Clothing Choices
  - ✓ Look online or bring examples; see Chapter 6
  - ✓ Computer with Internet access (if needed)
- ✯ Chart paper & Markers
- ✯ Name tags
- ✯ **Handouts**
  - ✓ Keep A Journal!
  - ✓ Phenomenal Woman by Maya Angelou
  - ✓ Help Us Improve! Week 2
  - ✓ Optional: Food Guide (Canada Food Guide or USDA Food Pyramid)

Last Week's Homework: Read Respect, Chapters 2 & 3, bring in a teen magazine

Run Time
90 min

Activity 1: Icebreaker – Human Knot	**10/10 min**

- ✯ If group > 8, divide into 2 or more groups
- ✯ Standing in a circle, group members reach across & shake hands
- ✯ Use your other hand to connect to a different person
- ✯ Challenge: Unravel human knot by unthreading bodies; Don't let go of hands

Activity 2: Checking In From Last Week	**5/15 min**

- ✯ Ask: *Any problems or questions from last week?*
- ✯ ***Do you like the book?*** Even when you disagree, it makes you think

GRG WEEK 2
Your Mind & Your Body

Activity 3: Your Mind (Respect, Chapter 2)　　　　　　　　　　　　　　**15/30 min**

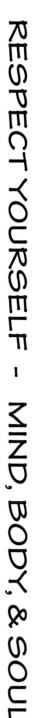

- ✩ **Respect starts on inside**
- ✩ **Self-respect shows on the outside**. Ask: *How?* (let participants speak first)

  - ✓ How you dress
  - ✓ Friends you choose – BF & GF
  - ✓ What you eat
  - ✓ How you take care of your body
  - ✓ Attitude towards school & work (now & later; babysitting, volunteer or paid)
  - ✓ How you talk **to** yourself & **about** yourself
  - ✓ Acting confident
  - ✓ Respect what others think but make up your own mind
  - ✓ Challenges you accept or back away from – healthy challenges!
    - ▪ Try out for team, lead a club, take a hard course, learn new language
  - ✓ Not afraid to show your talent
    - ▪ Don't dumb yourself down
  - ✓ Change friends if your friends don't support you or treat you respectfully
  - ✓ Set boundaries: don't let others treat you or touch you in ways you don't like

- ✩ **False Self vs. True Self** (Respect, p 21)

- ✩ Ask for Definition:
  - ✓ **False Self:** self you show the world
  - ✓ **True Self**: self inside
- ✩ Let's call it **Outer vs. Inner Self** (but it's not how you look)

GRG WEEK 2
Your Mind & Your Body

Activity 3: Your Mind (continued...)   **15/30 min**

✩ **Inner Self:**

- ✓ How you act around your family
- ✓ How you act when you're totally comfortable
- ✓ How you feel inside
- ✓ We can change over time

✩ **When is Outer Self different from Inner Self?**

- ✓ Embarrassed or afraid to look bad or be judged
- ✓ Please others or not let others down
- ✓ Be who you think you **should** be or others want you to be
- ✓ Easier to do what's more popular or accepted
- ✓ To make friends
- ✓ To impress a boy
- ✓ To make people notice you

✩ Careful not to believe stereotypes of who girls are or what they can (or can't) do

✩ **Stereotype:** *A formula, simplification, or a generalization used to paint a quick mental picture of a person, a group, or a behavior. Stereotypes can be used to give a fast snapshot, but there's a big risk a stereotype can oversimplify, be restrictive, prejudiced, or show a lack of critical thinking.*

The media uses stereotypes a lot. Watch your favorite TV shows: Are the people with glasses generally smart? Are taller people more successful? Are women more focused on relationships and men more on work?   **Source:** *Chris Fraser*

- ✓ **Stereotypes can restrict & limit**
- ✓ **We stay inside boxes other people build for us**

GRG WEEK 2
Your Mind & Your Body

Activity 3: Your Mind (continued...)   **15/30 min**

- ✓ **What are examples of limiting ideas about girls or women?**
    - ⇨ Physical or athletic ability ("girls can't throw a ball")
    - ⇨ Intellectual or school ability ("dumb blonde")
    - ⇨ Emotional strength ("girls cry, boys don't")
    - ⇨ Career choices ("girls can't be doctors or bosses")
    - ⇨ Expressing yourself vs being quiet & "obedient"
    - ⇨ Girls have PMS ("are you PMSing?")
    - ⇨ Effect of commercials – Ex: Hair care products, makeup

- ✓ We can end up limiting **ourselves**, not even realizing **we've accepted someone else's ideas of who we should be or could be**

Activity 4: Journaling (Respect, p 23)   **10/40 min**
Handout: Keep A Journal!

- ✩ Sometimes, we listen too much to ideas of who we should be, from outside us
- ✩ **Sometimes, we haven't looked inside enough to know our Inner Self**
    - ✓ How we really feel
    - ✓ What we really like
    - ✓ What are our strengths & weaknesses

- ✩ **Keeping A Journal**
    - ✓ Good way to get in touch with Inner Self
    - ✓ Try it for a week
    - ✓ Different types of journals; Some journals personal & confidential; others fine to share; share what you want for next week; respect each other's confidentiality

GRG WEEK 2
Your Mind & Your Body

Activity 4: Journaling (continued...)   **10/40 min**
Handout: Keep A Journal!

✩ **Keep A Journal!** Open to Respect, **"Pencil Yourself In"**, p 23

- ✓ **Start:** Make list of 10-20 passions; **Do this now**
    - ⇨ Things you love to do & why
    - ⇨ List a few you want to try
- ✓ **Day 2-6**: Keep a log of what you do each day & for how long
- ✓ **Day 7** (before we meet next): Compare passions to log. Similar? Different?

    Write in your log:
    - ⇨ Stars around activities you love
    - ⇨ Circle "can't skip" responsibilities
    - ⇨ Underline "don't enjoy" or "distractions"
        - Ex: *too much* Facebook, TV, etc

✩ **Set A Goal**

- ✓ Pick 1 activity you'd like to do more of, get better at, or find out about
- ✓ Make a plan to explore it
- ✓ Read "Road Trip" (Respect, p 24)
- ✓ Do 1 **small** thing every day towards that goal (Internet research, 1 phone call, write 1 paragraph)
- ✓ Break it down
- ✓ List any steps towards that goal in your journal this week

> **"Your past is not your potential.
> In any hour you can choose to liberate the future"**
>
> ... *Marilyn Ferguson*

GRG WEEK 2
Your Mind & Your Body

Activity 5: Respectful Self-Talk   5/45 min

- We can be our own worst enemies
- **Pretend you are your own best friend** – Would you talk to her that way?
- **Speak the way you would speak to her (him),** *especially* **when you make a mistake or things aren't going well**
- **Catch yourself when you slip up and change it; Takes practice**
- If you say something to yourself long enough or often enough it will come true
- If you tell yourself you're stupid, eventually you will be
- **Keep 1 week log of all positive and negative self-talk in your journal**
- **"If you think you can or you think you can't, you're right"**
  Henry Ford (1st CEO Ford Auto)

Activity 6: Your Body   10/55 min
Materials: Stars Without Makeup Pictures

- Physical beauty comes in all shapes and sizes
- Popular image of "what's beautiful" changes every 5-10 years
- Pressure today to fit into a narrow definition of beauty
- Often unrealistic
- Even the stars don't look that good without lights, hair, makeup, & wardrobe
- **Stars Without Makeup Pictures**
  List of websites, print & show examples, & discuss
  - ✓ **Here In Reality:** *hereinreality.com/makeup*
  - ✓ **ABC News:** *abcnews.go.com/entertainment/popup?id=4577150*
  - ✓ **Top Socialite:** *topsocialite.com/celebrities-without-makeup*

> I am powerful
> I am worthy
> I am loveable
> I am free

GRG WEEK 2
Your Mind & Your Body

Activity 6: Your Body (continued...) **10/55 min**
Materials: Stars Without Makeup Pictures

- **They're perfectly lovely girls & women – just like us!**
- **A self-respecting girl or woman is beautiful, no matter outer shape or size**
- Inner beauty is permanent, outer beauty changes
- Ask: **What gives you inner beauty?**
    - Confidence
    - Compassion – concern for others
    - Curiosity
    - Humor
    - Strength
    - Resilience – bouncing back
    - Gentleness

Activity 7: Making Body Choices **20/75 min**
Materials: Celebrities' Clothing Choices Pictures

- **Choice: How You Think About Your Body** (Respect, p 38)
    - ✓ Many of us have distorted ideas about weight & size
    - ✓ Only 9% of high school girls are overweight but 36% think they are. Why?
    - ✓ What are negative things that girls think about their bodies?
    - ✓ **We're really critical of our bodies. Why?**
        - Another example of negative self-talk
        - Unrealistic standards to be perfect
        - Huge media influence (print & video)
        - Criticism from friends and family
        - Pressure to be the same as everyone else

GRG Week 2   91

GRG WEEK 2
Your Mind & Your Body

Activity 7: Making Body Choices (continued...) **20/75 min**
Materials: Celebrities' Clothing Choices Pictures

- ✓ **How can we think about our bodies respectfully?**
    - ♥ Don't compare yourself to others
    - ♥ Have patience:
      Bodies keep changing until you're in your 20s
    - ♥ Think about what your body does for you:
      Strength to do everything you need it to
    - ♥ Need to keep it healthy, powerful, & strong

Your Body
Stay Healthy
Stay Powerful
Stay Strong

- ☆ **Choice: How You Look & Dress** (Respect, p 39)

    - ✓ **What can you tell about someone from the clothes they wear?**
        - Athletic? Sexy? Goth? Gangster? Scene? Preppy?
        - Dress like your friends or different? Individual style?
        - Labels – Hollister, American Eagle, Aritzia, Zara (pick current faves)
        - In high school, people don't want to dress all the same
        - Can wear *some* labels, on sale, find a balance

    - ✓ **Girls: how low, how tight, how short?**
        - Sexy vs. Over The Top? How can you tell?
        - Depends on event – dress differently to go out with your family, to school, to party
        - How do you decide?

    - ✓ Show **Celebrities' Clothing Choices Pictures**

    - ✓ What do they say with their clothing?
        - **Academy Awards 2008:**
          people.com/celebrity photos
        - **The Sun: Celebrity Style: Who, What, "Wear"**
          thesun.co.uk/sol/homepage/woman/fashion/article1090433.ece
        - **Search for** "celebrity fashions", "celebrity clothing", etc.

Celebrity Style

GRG WEEK 2
Your Mind & Your Body

Optional Activity (time permitting):

Activity 8: Nutrition – Respect For Your Body (Respect, p 39)   **10 min**
Handout: Food Guide (Canada Food Guide or USDA Food Pyramid)
Leaders: Order free Food Guide reprints from the appropriate government office

---

☆ **Choice: How You Feed Your Body**
  Note: This is usually covered in health class in school, but it's great to cover it from a respect-based perspective, if you have time

  ✓ **How do we make smart food choices?**

  ✓ **Hard to make good choices if you don't know about nutrition**

  ✓ Eating too much? Eating too little? Eating the wrong things?

  ✓ Every body has slightly different metabolism – how fast you burn calories

  - Body shape & size
  - Gender
  - How much muscle vs. how much fat on your body
  - How much exercise

  ✓ Every body will have a different need for calories

  - A male teen athlete may need 4,000 calories per day
  - A female teen non-athlete may need 2,000

  ✓ Make sure you know what you need

  ✓ **Not just calories – it's the building blocks: Protein, carbs, fat, & water**

  ✓ **Need some of each at every meal for enough energy to get through the day**

  ✓ Have you learned about nutrition in health class?

  ✓ **Hand out Food Guide.** Could do whole unit on Food Guide; give website info

  ✓ **[Be prepared for questions about eating disorders. Talk about this in meeting prep with your Adult Advisors]**

GRG WEEK 2
Your Mind & Your Body

Optional Activity (time permitting):

Activity 8: Nutrition – Respect For Your Body (Respect, p 39) **10 min**
Handout: Food Guide (Canada Food Guide or USDA Food Pyramid)

☆ **Choice: How You Move** (Respect, p 41)

  ✓ Ask: **Why do we need exercise?**

   ⇨ Keep heart strong
   ⇨ Build strength & muscle
   ⇨ Strong muscle keeps bones strong
   ⇨ Control stress
   ⇨ Improve your mood
   ⇨ Burn off extra calories

  ✓ **Exercise releases "feel-good" brain chemicals** (serotonin & endorphins)

   ▪ Do you get enough? At least 30 min 3x a week
   ▪ What kind of exercise do you like?
   ▪ Make it something fun – you'll do it
   ▪ Try something new & be patient. You'll get better as you learn
   ▪ Do it with your friends
   ▪ Do it with music – ipod, mp3
   ▪ Get some sun (improves your mood, esp. in winter)

Activity 9: Phenomenal Woman by Maya Angelou **5/80 min**
Handout: Phenomenal Woman – Take turns reading aloud

> "Do not bother just to be better than your contemporaries or predecessors. Try to be better than yourself"
>
> … William Faulkner

GRG WEEK 2
Your Mind & Your Body

Activity 10: Fill In Help Us Improve! & GRG Garden 10/90 min
Handout: Help Us Improve! Week 2

For Next Week:

- Read Respect, Chapter 4, Your Media IQ
- Keep A Journal! exercise
- 1 week log of all positive & negative self-talk
- Bring in a teen magazine
- Think of or find a picture of 1 positive role model & 1 negative role model
- For each picture, write down why you think they're a role model
    - ✓ 1-2 things you admire about them
    - ✓ 1-2 things you don't admire about them

GRG WEEK 2
Keep A Journal!
Get In Touch With Your Inner Self

See Respect, "Pencil Yourself In", p 23

Journaling: Getting Started

✧ Try it for a week

✧ Different types of journals

　⇨ Some are personal & confidential, others fine to share

　⇨ Share what you want for next week; respect each other's confidentiality

✧ **Start:** Make list of 10-20 passions

　⇨ Things you love to do & why

　⇨ List a few you want to try

✧ **Day 2-6:** Keep a log of what you do each day & for how long

✧ **Day 7** (before we meet next time): Compare your passions to your log

　⇨ Similar? Different?

In your log:
　⇨ Stars around activities you love

　⇨ Circle "can't skip" responsibilities

　⇨ Underline "don't enjoy" or "distractions" (too much Facebook, TV, etc)

Set A Goal

✧ Pick 1 activity you'd like to do more of, get better at, or find out about

✧ Make a plan to explore it

✧ Read "Road Trip" (Respect, p 24)

✧ Do 1 **small** thing every day towards that goal (Internet research, 1 phone call, write 1 paragraph, etc); break it down

✧ List any steps towards that goal in your journal this week

✧ Report back to us next week!

From: Macavinta, Courtney and Vander Pluym, Andrea. *Respect: A Girl's Guide to Getting Respect & Dealing When Your Line is Crossed.* Minneapolis: Free Spirit Publishing, 2005.

Phenomenal Woman
Maya Angelou

Pretty women wonder where my secret lies.
I'm not cute or built to suit a fashion model's size
But when I start to tell them,
They think I'm telling lies.

I say,
It's in the reach of my arms
The span of my hips,
The stride of my step,
The curl of my lips.
I'm a woman
Phenomenally.
Phenomenal woman,
That's me.

I walk into a room
Just as cool as you please,
And to a man,
The fellows stand or
Fall down on their knees.
Then they swarm around me,
A hive of honey bees.

I say,
It's the fire in my eyes,
And the flash of my teeth,
The swing in my waist,
And the joy in my feet.
I'm a woman
Phenomenally.
Phenomenal woman,
That's me.

Men themselves have wondered
What they see in me.
They try so much
But they can't touch
My inner mystery.
When I try to show them,
They say they still can't see.

I say,
It's in the arch of my back,
The sun of my smile,
The ride of my breasts,
The grace of my style.
I'm a woman
Phenomenally.
Phenomenal woman,
That's me.

Now you understand
Just why my head's not bowed.
I don't shout or jump about
Or have to talk real loud.
When you see me passing
It ought to make you proud.

I say,
It's in the click of my heels,
The bend of my hair,
The palm of my hand,
The need for my care,
'Cause I'm a woman
Phenomenally.
Phenomenal woman,
That's me.

© 1978 Maya Angelou. Reprinted with permission

Help Us Improve!!

GRG WEEK 2
Your Mind & Your Body

What 3 Ideas Or Activities Did You Like Best This Week?

1.

2.

3.

Anything We Should Cut? Or Improve?

1.

2.

3.

Other Comments? Your Ideas Help Us A Lot!! Thanks!

CHAPTER 9
GRG WEEK 3
Your Media IQ

Reference Material: Respect, Chapter 4

Class Materials:

- Dove Evolution video – look up online: **campaignforrealbeauty.com** or search for "Dove Evolution" on **youtube.com**
- Mean Girls movie
- Influences & Identity Video
- TV with DVD player or computer with speakers for playing DVDs
- Teen magazines (1 for each girl, in case participants forget)
- Chart paper & Markers
- Name tags
- **Handouts**
  - ✓ Help Us Improve! Week 3

Last Week's Homework:

- Read Respect, Chapter 4
- Leaders: Prepare stories from your own experience about "popular" kids at your school & the difference between middle & high school
- Keep A Journal!
- Self-talk log
- Bring in a teen magazine
- Think of or find a picture of 1 positive role model & 1 negative role model
- For each picture, write down why you think they're a role model

Run Time
90 min

Activity 1: Icebreaker – Group Stand Up	10/10 min

- Group sits in a tight circle, facing outwards. Link arms, attempt to stand
- Use teamwork & help each other

GRG WEEK 3
Your Media IQ

Activity 2: Checking In From Last Week   5/15 min

✩ Ask: Are you seeing things differently? Has GRG changed anything for you?

✩ **Homework**

  ✓ **Journal**: discuss homework; progress towards goal

  ✓ Are you doing things you hadn't realized?

  ✓ **Self-Talk Log**: what did you learn about yourself?

  ✓ **Role Models**: Discuss; Everybody is a mix of things we DO & DON'T like

✩ What did you like about Chapter 4? Dislike? Disagree?

Activity 3: Media Overload (open to Respect, p 50, Teen magazines)   15/30 min

---

✩ Did you know? **$13 billion** spent yearly by ad companies & commercials targeted at teens

✩ Read the story of Monique & Ines (ee-nez) (Respect, p 50)

✩ Have you ever felt the media was telling you how you should act and look? Examples?

✩ **Indirect Messages:**

  ✓ Buy this product and life will be perfect (boys & girls will notice)

  ✓ Your life will be terrible without it

✩ Normal to be curious, learn from others, grow & change

✩ Have you ever wanted the life, clothes, face, body, boyfriend of characters on popular TV shows? (America's Next Top Model, OC, The Hills, Gossip Girls, pick current shows)

✩ **Ever felt you didn't measure up after watching TV or reading magazines?**

✩ **Advertisers try to make you believe you need "right stuff" to be popular**

  ✓ Clothes, purse, sunglasses, makeup, hair products

  ✓ Pay teens as consultants to use their brands to start trends

GRG WEEK 3
Your Media IQ

Activity 3: Media Overload (continued...)   **15/30 min**

- ✯ **Product Placement Game**
  - ✓ Watch a movie or TV show
  - ✓ How many name brand products can you spot?
  - ✓ Movie companies paid to show those products; Train yourself to see them

- ✯ **Can Anyone Be Perfect?**
  - ✓ **Constant comparison hurts self-esteem; undermines your self-respect**
  - ✓ Ask someone to read Respect, p 52, Karinna's comment (in bubble): *"We're constantly being told we're not good enough – from clothes, to relationships, to what we do on the weekends. The media shows us that we have to be this cool, ultimate girl."*
  - ✓ Do you agree with Karinna?
  - ✓ **Without realizing, media's messages slowly influence you, friends, family**

- ✯ **Big Question**: **How do we find balance & keep ourselves strong & not be too influenced by negative media influences???**
  - ✓ **1st Step: Become aware that you're being manipulated**
  - ✓ All: Find 2 magazine ads that illustrate this

Activity 4: Fiction, Myth, & Lies (Respect, p 53)   **40/70 min**
Materials: Dove video, Mean Girls movie

- ✯ **Myth 1: You Can Never Be Too Thin Or Pretty**
  - ✓ **Dove Evolution** video
  - ✓ Did you realize magazines & ad companies go so far to change models' looks?
  - ✓ Can anyone really look like that?
  - ✓ How does it make you feel?
  - ✓ Will it change how you look at other ads?

GRG WEEK 3
Your Media IQ

Activity 4: Fiction, Myth, & Lies (continued...)   **40/70 min**

Materials: Dove video, Mean Girls movie

☆ **Myth 2: You Must Be Popular**

- ✓ **Mean Girls** movie
- ✓ **Myth: You have to be mean to be cool or popular**
- ✓ Open to Respect, p 57, Sisterhood box; Read out loud
- ✓ Watch **Mean Girls** Lunchroom Scene, Scene 3, 13:38-15:22
   - ⇨ How many Respect Basics are violated?
   - ⇨ Notice product placements
- ✓ **Ask: What does "popular" mean to you?**
   - ⇨ Someone who is friends with most people, nice, & friendly?
   - ⇨ Someone who cuts people down? Everyone fears? Intimidating?
   - ⇨ What are your experiences? (**Each Leader share a story**)
   - ⇨ High School vs Elementary School popularity
- ✓ **Why is promoting mean girls' popularity so bad?** (*Clueless, Mean Girls*)
- ✓ Do these girls have respect for each other or themselves? Why or why not?

Myth: Life Is Super Sexy

☆ **Myth 3: You Need To Find Mr. Right**

- ✓ Eventually, you'll be interested in romantic relationships
- ✓ Important to have boys as friends and work partners 1st
- ✓ Too much emphasis on dating & romance
- ✓ Figure out who **you** are 1st
- ✓ Then you'll know what kind of person you want as BF or GF
- ✓ With self-respect, you're more attractive to you & everyone around you
- ✓ You'll attract the right people to you

GRG WEEK 3
Your Media IQ

Activity 4: Fiction, Myth, & Lies (continued...)   **40/70 min**

Materials: Dove video, Mean Girls movie

- **Myth 4: Life Is Super Sexy**

- **Myth 5: Females Are Eye Candy Or Victims**

  - ✓ Music videos: How are women portrayed?
  - ✓ TV Shows: Flava of Love, That's Amore; use current examples
  - ✓ What roles do women & teens play on popular TV shows?
  - ✓ Stereotypes?
    - ⇨ Smart?
    - ⇨ Flirty?
    - ⇨ Hard working?
    - ⇨ What's most important to them?
    - ⇨ Do they treat their friends with respect?
    - ⇨ 1-dimensional characters

Myth: Females Are Eye Candy

Activity 5: Question What You See (Respect, p 60)   **10/80 min**

Materials: Influences & Identity video

- **Influences & Identity** by Alicia Mandic, YouTube video
  youtube.com/watch?v=tRDzyT3ogjE, or search for it on YouTube

- **Be aware of stereotypes & myths** behind what you see

- **Look for examples of real females** (read from list, Respect, p 61)

- **Look for motives** – dig a little deeper (read from list, Respect, p 61)

- **Set boundaries** – don't watch, read, or buy products disrespectful to women

- **Skip the commercials**

GRG WEEK 3
Your Media IQ

Activity 5: Question What You See (continued...)　　　　　　　　　　　　　　　**10/80 min**

✫ **Resources** (ask girls to write in their journals & look up before next week):

- ✓ Center For Media Literacy: **medialit.org**
- ✓ Turn Beauty Inside Out: **bio.org**
- ✓ New Moon Magazine: **newmoon.org**
- ✓ Campaign For Commercial-Free Childhood: **commercialfreechildhood.org**
- ✓ Girls Can Do Anything Magazine: **gcdamagazine.com**

Activity 6: Fill In Help Us Improve! & GRG Garden　　　　　　　　　　　　　　　**10/90 min**
Handout: Help Us Improve! Week 3

For Next Week:
Respect, Chapter 5, Family
Look up media websites

> **"Quitting is a habit. Every time you quit, you damage your self-esteem & send your psyche the message that you're incompetent. You are competent! Each time you take action & stick to your commitment when you felt like quitting, you'll gain a newfound confidence that makes the next step increasingly easier"**
>
> *... Cynthia Kersey*

Help Us Improve!!

GRG WEEK 3
Your Media IQ

What 3 Ideas Or Activities Did You Like Best This Week?

1.

2.

3.

Anything We Should Cut? Or Improve?

1.

2.

3.

Other Comments? Your Ideas Help Us A Lot!! Thanks!

CHAPTER 10
GRG WEEK 4
Family

Reference Material: Respect, Chapter 5

Class Materials:

- **Handouts:**
  - ✓ Help Us Improve! Week 4
- Chart paper & Markers (4 boxes)
- Scrap paper

Last Week's Homework: Read Respect, Chapter 5, Look up media websites

Run Time
90 min

Activity 1: Icebreaker – Communication Games   5/05 min

Sorting Game

- Girls line up
- Without talking, arrange themselves by:
  - ✓ Birthday
  - ✓ Alphabetical order (first name)

Or: Pieces Of Ourselves

- Each girl take out 2-3 pieces of scrap paper
- For each piece of paper, share 1 important fact about yourself
- Share something important about who you are
  - ✓ Important: likes, dislikes, goals (not just hair color)

*"The key to realizing a dream is to focus
not on success but on significance.
Then even the small steps & little victories along your path
will take on a greater meaning"*

... Oprah Winfrey

GRG WEEK 4
Family

Activity 2: Checking In From Last Week   5/10 min

- Discuss any ideas that have come up through the week
- Have you noticed any changes in your reactions to situations? Describe
- Are you standing up for yourself more (in a polite & kind way)?
- Are you journaling?
- Media websites from last week
- Are you watching TV differently?

Activity 3: What Is A Family?   10/20 min

- Note: We use **parent** as a general term to represent:
  - ✓ 2 parents living in the same house with you
  - ✓ 1 parent
  - ✓ 2 parents living separately
  - ✓ 1 parent & 1 stepparent
  - ✓ Legal guardian
  - ✓ Foster parent
  - ✓ Other ideas?

- **What does family mean to you? What's special about your family?**
- **What do you believe is necessary for a happy & successful family?**

Activity 4: Your Rights Within The Family   5/25 min

- **Your rights within your family are similar to your personal rights**
- **What do you believe your rights within your family are?** (Respect, p 79)
  - ✓ To feel like you belong
  - ✓ To feel like you are equal
  - ✓ To be and feel independent

108   Girls' Respect Groups

GRG WEEK 4
Family

Activity 4: Your Rights Within The Family (continued...) **5/25 min**

- ✓ To listen to your feelings
- ✓ To follow your passions
- ✓ To be the real you
- ✓ To speak and change your mind
- ✓ To be different from your family
- ✓ To be respected in general

✩ **Realities of life**

- ✓ We still need to listen to parents
- ✓ Parents need to listen to kids
- ✓ All families have disagreements
- ✓ Every family has things they can do better

FAMILY FEUD

Activity 5: Communication **20/45 min**

✩ Do you & your family members ever fight? ☺ Is there a family that doesn't??

✩ What do you fight about most often?

✩ Note to Leaders: Encourage different examples of fight types & resolution ideas

✩ **How to resolve fights respectfully & without damage?** (open to Respect, p 73)

- ✓ **Speak up** about what's bothering you! Use your voice – with respect
- ✓ **Prepare** for the discussion. Think about what you want to say & how to say it in a positive, convincing way
- ✓ **Keep it a discussion**, not a fight. You can **really disagree**, without fighting
- ✓ **Be fair.** Stay on topic. No "You Always" or "You Never". Don't bring up the past 10 things that are bugging you
- ✓ Once you've handled this discussion successfully, you can bring up the past 10 things … 1 at a time! And don't wait so long or keep troubles stuffed inside. It makes you blow up at the little things!

GRG WEEK 4
Family

Activity 5: Communication (continued...)　　　　　　　　**20/45 min**

- ✓ Use an **open, positive tone of voice & body language**. No hands on hips, eye rolling, or whining. Parents hate that, even if your idea is good

- ✓ When a parent is talking, **listen** (shows respect, even if you disagree)

- ✓ **Let them know you've heard their message**.
  This doesn't mean you agree, just that you understand.
  "I see what you're saying", "You've got a good point" (if you think so)

- ✓ **Compromise & be flexible**
  Give a little to get some of what you want, now & later

☆ **Other ideas to try:**
  - ✓ **Give them an opportunity to trust you**

  - ✓ **Be respectful**

  - ✓ Honestly try to **understand their POV** (Point Of View) – ask questions

  - ✓ **Stay calm**. Take a break to avoid big argument. Return when everyone's cooler

  - ✓ **Recognize their concerns** and try to address them in your response

  - ✓ **Be honest!**

☆ **Remember: You cannot change others. You can only change yourself**
  - ✓ **If you change and stick with it, eventually people will notice**

  - ✓ **If you change, the people around you will change the way they treat you**

☆ **Understanding Parents' Point Of View (POV)**
  - ✓ How do your parents feel about you growing up & being more independent?

  - ✓ What are they are worried about? Why?

  - ✓ What's your bedtime? Do your parents enforce it?

  - ✓ How much time do you spend on the computer?

  - ✓ How often does your family eat dinner together?

  - ✓ Why do you think your parents do these things?

  - ✓ Do you think your parents feel sad or anxious about being needed less?

GRG WEEK 4
Family

Activity 5: Communication (continued...)   **20/45 min**

✩ **Understanding Parents' Point Of View (POV)** (continued...)

- ✓ Have they ever said so?
- ✓ How could they express these fears in a better way?
  - ⇨ Talk to you about them
  - ⇨ Share their childhood experiences:
    (Helps you avoid learning lessons the hard way)

Activity 6: Keeping Your Cool During Fights (Respect, p 76)   **10/55 min**

✩ **Say what's bothering you without eye rolling or door slamming**

✩ **Stay calm**

✩ **Focus on the endpoint**. What do you want? Will acting angry get you there?

✩ **No yelling**

✩ **Hold smart comments**.
It's tough, but pushing others' buttons won't get what you want

✩ **Breathe!** (seriously, this lowers your body's stress chemicals!)

✩ **Recognize & identify your feelings**

✩ **Listen**. How is the other person feeling?

✩ **Take a 30 min break** when things get too hot

✩ **Write a letter** or e-mail expressing your feelings
- ✓ Is it mean or just venting? Throw it out, don't send it
- ✓ If it's calm, expresses feelings & suggests a solution, send it
- ✓ Might have to write both!

✩ Other ideas that work for you?

GRG WEEK 4
Family

Activity 7: Siblings 10/65 min

- **Siblings: Best friends, worst enemies**
- Go around table. Identify your sibling role – oldest, middle, youngest, single
- Older vs. younger siblings (being & having): + and -
- **Ideas for living peacefully with siblings:**
  - Respect their property & feelings; More likely they'll respect yours
  - Don't compete
  - Don't put them down
  - Be happy & proud of their accomplishments
- **Stepsiblings**: Accept them for who they are; you can't change them
  - Set respectful boundaries and limits for yourself & them
  - Don't play 1 parent off against the other (I'll go to my Mom's house); drives the stepsiblings & all the parents crazy!
- These things are true for non-blended families, too!

Sisters

Activity 8: Family Relationship Recipe 15/80 min

- Make 3 groups: Each group is a different family member (Sibs, Mom, Dad)
- Each group write down the ideal characteristics or traits of that family member (not my Mom, but Moms in general, for example)
- Arrange them in order of importance
- Allow 8 min for groups to brainstorm
- Return to table & review results with all groups. Ask everyone to add to the lists
- Briefly discuss if their family members have these characteristics
- **Ask myself: Do I have these characteristics? How can I grow into them?**

GRG WEEK 4
Family

Activity 9: Change Takes Time   5/85 min

- **Don't expect immediate results!**
- **Even when you change, it takes a while for the people around you to realize that you've changed & for them to change, too** (3 months!)
- **Be patient!**
- **Keep at it.** It can take 10 tries, but the results are worth it

Activity 10: Fill In Help Us Improve! & GRG Garden   5/90 min
Handout: Help Us Improve! Week 4

For Next Week:
Read Respect, Chapters 6 & 11, Friends & Fighting For Your Rights At School

Help Us Improve!!

GRG WEEK 4
Family

What 3 Ideas Or Activities Did You Like Best This Week?

1.

2.

3.

Anything We Should Cut? Or Improve?

1.

2.

3.

Other Comments? Your Ideas Help Us A Lot!! Thanks!

CHAPTER 11
GRG WEEK 5
Friends & Fighting For Your Rights At School

Reference Material: Respect, Chapters 6 & 11
Class Materials:

- Chart paper & Markers
- **Handouts**
  - Why You *Should* Gossip (2 pgs)
  - Help Us Improve! Week 5
  - Parent Notice: Next week GRG is 10 min longer (110 min)

Last Week's Homework: Read Respect, Chapters 6 & 11

Run Time
95 min

Activity 1: Icebreaker – Floor Clap 5/05 min

- Everyone kneels on floor in a circle (can sit at table)
- Hands palms down on the floor (table)
- Put your R hand on far side of the L hand of person next to you (all hands still on floor/table); everyone's hands are alternating
- Initiator taps the table once. The tap travels around the circle
- If someone taps twice, it reverses
- If you mess the rhythm up, you take out your hand
- Objective: Be the last person with your hand still in

Activity 2: Checking In From Last Week 5/10 min

- Discuss ideas that came up through the week
- Have you noticed any changes in your reactions to situations?
- Are you standing up for yourself more (in a polite & kind way)?
- Are you journaling?

GRG WEEK 5
Friends & Fighting For Your Rights At School

Activity 3: Friendship Types — 10/20 min

- ✰ **Friendships:** Ask: *What's the difference between...?*
  - ✓ Average friendships
  - ✓ Superficial friendships
  - ✓ Mean Girls (frenemies)
  - ✓ Trustworthy friends
  - ✓ Sisterhood
  - ✓ What are the signs of a good friend?

Activity 4: Making Friends — 10/30 min

- ✰ **Be Yourself**
- ✰ **Be Caring**
- ✰ **Be Honest**
- ✰ **Be There For Your Friends**
  - ✓ Don't take them for granted; Help them when they need it
  - ✓ Go to their important events (performances, awards)
  - ✓ Be there in difficult times (disappointments, losses)
- ✰ **Be Inclusive**
- ✰ **Look For Shared Interests & Ideas** – things in common
- ✰ **Be Open To New Friends**
- ✰ **Be Dependable**
- ✰ **Ask**: *Which of these are hardest to follow? Which are the easiest?*
  - ✓ Do you worry people won't like you if you're "just" yourself?
  - ✓ Do we take our friends for granted after a long time?
  - ✓ Why is making room for new friends so hard? What can we do better?

BE TRUE TO YOURSELF

GRG WEEK 5
Friends & Fighting For Your Rights At School

Activity 4: Making Friends (continued...)   **10/30 min**

- ✓ Can you put your trust in someone who once betrayed you?
    - ⇨ Telling a secret
    - ⇨ Gossiping about you to a friend
- ✓ What if it's all 1-sided?
    - ⇨ Ex: Your "friend" doesn't return your calls; doesn't invite you
- ✭ Which of these things show lack of caring? Which can be overlooked?

Activity 5: Positive & Negative Things To Do With Friends   **5/35 min**

- 💣 "Burn Book" (Mean Girls)
- 💣 Gossip
- 💣 Putting Others Down/Ganging Up
- ♥ 💣 MSN (could be good or bad)
- ♥ 💣 Facebook (could be good or bad)
- ♥ Hanging Out
- ♥ Getting Ready To Go Out Together
- ♥ Doing Homework
- ♥ Going To Movies
- ♥ Shopping
- ♥ Talking About Boys

GOSSIP

GRG WEEK 5
Friends & Fighting For Your Rights At School

Activity 6: Gossip 10/45 min

Handout: *Shape* Magazine, Why You *Should* Gossip

- Hand out *Shape* article on girls' gossip (2 pgs: article & response form)
- Work in groups of 4 to write an e-mail back to *Shape* Magazine
- Do you agree or disagree? Is it good for girls to gossip to build friendships? Why?
- Example of **Critical Thinking**: Don't accept everything you read, hear, or see

Activity 7: Disrespect Dilemmas (open to Respect, p 94) **15/60 min**

- Go around room; read these 10 ideas & give examples (Leaders add own)

Activity 8: Role Play – Friendship Rx (open to Respect, p 96) **10/70 min**

- Girls pair up & pick 1 Friendship Rx situation
- Each pair acts out both a positive & negative way to solve the problem

Activity 9: How To End A Friendship (Respect, p 98) **5/75 min**

- Don't discuss, but these are good tips for preparing yourself to end a friendship

> "We learn wisdom from failure much more than from success; we often discover what will do, by finding out what will not do and probably she who never made a mistake never made a discovery"
>
> ... Samuel Smiles

GRG WEEK 5
Friends & Fighting For Your Rights At School

Activity 10: Standing Up For Your Rights (Respect, p 169)　　　　15/90 min

---

- ✯ **Sexual Harassment**
  - ✓ Taunts
  - ✓ Looks, Gestures
  - ✓ Rumors
  - ✓ Exposure To Explicit Images
  - ✓ Unwanted Touching Or Physical Contact

- ✯ **Ask:** *Have you ever seen someone being sexually harassed?*
  - ✓ How did the people involved deal with it? Did any bystanders help?
  - ✓ Obvious or Subtle; Actions or Words
  - ✓ Subtle Examples:
    - ⇨ Standing too close
    - ⇨ Guys saying "rape" as an everyday expression desensitizes it
    - ⇨ "I owned you" (in a sports game), "You're screwed" or worse
  - ✓ **What about these sayings demeans people as a whole?**
  - ✓ **What are some ways that sexual harassment is seen as acceptable?**
  - ✓ **What are the effects of guys being disrespectful to girls? Girls to guys?**
  - ✓ **What are the effects of girls being disrespectful to each other?**
  - ✓ **What makes harassment so hard to deal with?**
  - ✓ **Why do we let it happen & not say anything?**

- ✯ **Solutions**

  - ✓ **Ask:** *What can you do to help stop sexual harassment?*
  - ✓ **What will you do to stop it the next time you witness it?**
  - ✓ **Stress that it's not "ratting out" to tell someone older**

GRG WEEK 5
Friends & Fighting For Your Rights At School

Activity 10: Standing Up For Your Rights (continued...) **15/90 min**

- ✫ **Bullying (Non-Sexual Harassment)**

  - ✓ **Verbal, Physical & Relational Bullying (Including Cyberbullying)**

    - What does it look like? Sound like?
    - What do you do when it happens? Ignore it? Step in to support a friend?
    - How to stop it?
    - Why is being a bystander so bad? What message does it send?

- ✫ **How To Stop It** (open to Respect, p 173)

  - ✓ Set A Boundary: Pick 2 examples to read
  - ✓ Document It – who, when, where, what
  - ✓ Telling vs. Tattling: When to report it

    - Tattling: Gets someone into trouble
    - Telling: Gets someone out of trouble

Activity 11: Fill In Help Us Improve! & GRG Garden **5/95 min**
Handouts: Help Us Improve! Week 5, **Parent Notice: Next Week GRG is 110 min**

For Next Week: Read Chapter 7, Relationships

GRG WEEK 5
Why You Should Gossip

shape YOUR LIFE news

Why You SHOULD Gossip

It may sound so high school, but sharing a little snarky gossip at a party or by the water cooler turns out to be one of the most effective ways to cement a new friendship or work relationship, according to research from the University of Oklahoma. "It doesn't mean you have to disparage someone you know personally to form a bond", says study leader Jennifer Bosson, Ph.D. Dishing about celebrities or other public figures is just as effective.

Shape Magazine, November 2006
Reprinted with permission

GRG WEEK 5
*Why You **Should** Gossip*

Shape Magazine, November 2006

Write an e-mail back to Shape Magazine, saying what you thought about this article. Using what we've talked about, please list the reasons for your support or objections & give some other ideas. (Use the reverse side if needed)

Have Fun!

To: *Shape* Magazine

From: Me

Subject: Why You *Should* Gossip article, November 2006

Dear *Shape* Magazine:

Help Us Improve!!

GRG WEEK 5

Friends & Fighting For Your Rights At School

What 3 Ideas Or Activities Did You Like Best This Week?

1.

2.

3.

Anything We Should Cut? Or Improve?

1.

2.

3.

Other Comments? Your Ideas Help Us A Lot!! Thanks!

CHAPTER 12
GRG WEEK 6
Romantic Relationships, Review, & Wrap Up

Reference Material: Respect, Chapter 7

✯ **Handouts**:
  ✓ Smart Girl's Guide To Boys (also bring a copy of the book to show)
  ✓ Respect Essentials
  ✓ Help Us Improve! Week 6
  ✓ Girls' Respect Group Wrap Up
  ✓ Keep It Going! (farewell message)

Last Week's Homework: Read Respect, Chapter 7

Leaders:

✯ You'll need fast access to a copy machine at the end of the session, to copy the girls' completed GRG Garden ideas. If you don't have access to a copier, ask the girls if it's ok to take the Garden handouts home with you, copy them, & return them to the school.

✯ We really like the book **A Smart Girl's Guide To Boys** from the American Girl collection. We suggest you order a copy to bring to Week 6 to pass around. It's a great resource for the girls to buy for themselves. There are fun discussions & activities for GRG that you can start from this book. We like the whole American Girl book collection. Check it out!

Run Time 110 min

Activity 1: What Is A Romantic Relationship? 5/05 min

✯ **What is a Romantic Relationship?**

✯ When 2 people _____ each other AND each other's thoughts & feelings
  ✓ Like/Love
  ✓ Trust
  ✓ Respect

✯ What does that look like? Examples?

GRG WEEK 6
Romantic Relationships, Review, & Wrap Up

Activity 2: When Am I Ready?   10/15 min

- ✩ Trust myself – Don't be pressured into it
- ✩ Everyone's ready at a different time
- ✩ Do my homework 1st – What kind of person do I like?
  - ✓ Respect Basics
  - ✓ Common Interests
  - ✓ Common Experiences
  - ✓ Common Outlook On Life
  - ✓ Set Your Boundaries
  - ✓ What Would Be The "Deal-Breakers"?
  - ✓ Hard To Know Till You're There
  - ✓ Do Your "Homework" (think about it in advance): helps you see the right person

Activity 3: Like, Trust, & Respect – The Basics   15/30 min

- ✩ Everything MUST be mutual (goes both ways; shared)
- ✩ I like you + you like me
- ✩ I trust you + you trust me
- ✩ I respect you + you respect me
- ✩ Doesn't mean you have to do everything together or agree on everything

- ✩ **Like Or Love**
  - ✓ **Ask**: *What do we mean by "like" or "love" romantically?*
  - ✓ Admire someone for what's on the inside (beliefs, dreams, thoughts, opinions)
  - ✓ Not just popularity or looks
  - ✓ Not crushing or infatuation – short-lived feeling for someone you barely know
  - ✓ Care about each other as friends, too

GRG WEEK 6
Romantic Relationships, Review, & Wrap Up

Activity 3: Like, Trust, & Respect – The Basics (continued...)   15/30 min

- **Like Or Love** (continued...)
  - ✓ Accept each other
  - ✓ Don't want to change one another
  - ✓ You're not going to love anyone 100%
  - ✓ Can you accept them as they are?

- **Trust** – What do we mean by Trust?
  - ✓ Feel free & safe with each other
  - ✓ Confident you will get the respect you deserve
  - ✓ Honesty
  - ✓ Mistakes happen; Must rebuild, if possible
  - ✓ Admit & apologize (sincerely) when you have lied or hurt the other
  - ✓ Sometimes relationship is too damaged to rebuild
  - ✓ Must accept responsibility; Give & receive apology; Heal & move forward

- **Respect** - What do we mean by respect in romantic relationships?
  - ✓ Listen to each other
  - ✓ Set your own & respect each other's boundaries
  - ✓ Speak up (without fear)
  - ✓ Treated as an equal
  - ✓ **Remember, respect begins with you!**
    Set the tone for how others should treat you

> "You gain strength, experience & confidence by every experience where you really stop to look fear in the face.
> You must do the thing you cannot do"
>
> ... Eleanor Roosevelt

GRG WEEK 6
Romantic Relationships, Review, & Wrap Up

Activity 4: A Smart Girl's Guide To Boys   10/40 min

- ✩ Talk about value of book; where to get it
- ✩ **Discussion Questions**:
  - ✓ Are you starting to feel different about guys you've known for a long time?
  - ✓ How do you stay "normal" while starting to like guys or girls romantically?
    - Ask questions (activities, homework, interests, sports)
    - Tell a joke
    - Smile, don't laugh too much (relax, try not to be nervous!)

Activity 5: Relationship DOs & DON'Ts   10/50 min

- ✩ **DOs & DON'Ts** (open to Respect, p 108 & pick a few)
- ✩ **Disrespect Disguised As Drama** (open to Respect, p 109 & pick a few)
  - ✓ Can't Resolve Disagreements
  - ✓ Cheating – Seeing Someone Else On The Side
  - ✓ Lying
  - ✓ Ignoring You In Public
  - ✓ Yelling
  - ✓ Dissing Your Friends
  - ✓ Drama As A Substitute For Caring Or Excitement
  - ✓ Jealousy Or Over Control

Activity 6: Breaking Up & Moving On (BF & GF)   10/60 min

- ✩ Make your decision
- ✩ **OK to feel sad & know it's the right decision at the same time**
- ✩ **Act respectfully in breakup**

GRG WEEK 6
Romantic Relationships, Review, & Wrap Up

Activity 6: Breaking Up & Moving On (BF & GF) (continued...)   **10/60 min**

- ✰ **Be kind, Don't be cruel, Don't lie**
- ✰ **Go easy on each other; Still learning**
- ✰ **Don't flip-flop** – break up today, back together tomorrow
- ✰ **Make some time to be sad**
    - ✓ Put in perspective: Limit your sad thoughts (5-10 min/day)
    - ✓ Change your routine: Don't do things that purposefully remind you of the other person; you'll just make yourself upset
    - ✓ Surround yourself with friends

Activity 7: Review & Wrap Up   **20/80 min**
Handout: Respect Essentials

Which ideas meant the most to you? Ask for 1-2 ideas & comments on each item

- ✰ **The Basics Of Respect ....**
    - ⇨ Have Self-Respect
    - ⇨ Listen To Your Gut
    - ⇨ Set Boundaries
    - ⇨ Speak Up
    - ⇨ Build Relationships
    - ⇨ Fight For Equality
    - ⇨ Get Help
- ✰ **Your Rights: You've Got A Right To ....**
    - ⇨ Feel Like You Belong!
    - ⇨ Feel Like An Equal!
    - ⇨ Figure Out You!
    - ⇨ Listen To Your True Feelings!

GRG WEEK 6
Romantic Relationships, Review, & Wrap Up

Activity 7: Review & Wrap Up (continued...)   **20/80 min**
Handout: Respect Essentials

- ✩ **Your Rights: You've Got a Right To ….** (continued...)
    - ⇨ Be Different & Individual!
    - ⇨ Feel & Be Safe!
    - ⇨ Be Independent!
    - ⇨ Follow Your Passions!
    - ⇨ BE YOU!
- ✩ **Your Choices ….**
    - ⇨ How You Look & Dress
    - ⇨ How You Feed, Think About, & Take Care Of Your Body
    - ⇨ How You Treat Others
    - ⇨ How You Meet Your Obligations
    - ⇨ Ex: schoolwork, housework, keeping dates with friends
    - ⇨ How You Deal When Things Don't Work Out The Way You Want

Activity 8: GRG Wrap Up & Goodbye   **30/110 min**
Fill In Help Us Improve!, GRG Garden, & GRG Wrap Up
Handouts: Help Us Improve! Week 6, GRG Garden, & GRG Wrap Up

- ✩ **COPY GRG Garden Handouts** for Leaders to keep; Ask if ok with girls
- ✩ Share Roses & Thorns of GRG
- ✩ Thanks & Goodbyes

Keep
Girls' Respect Groups
Growing!

GRG WEEK 6

A Smart Girl's Guide To Boys

Surviving Crushes, Staying True To Yourself & Other Love Stuff

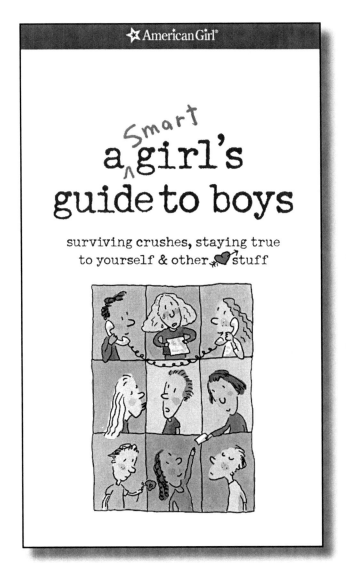

Author: Pleasant Company
Publisher: American Girl Publishing

For More Information:
www.AmericanGirl.com

From The Publisher:

Here's straight talk on what to do when everyone's wondering "who likes who?". Includes letters from girls and advice from boys on being friends, going out, getting dumped, and being yourself - plus tips and quizzes to get your brain back on track when your heart's in a wreck! Appropriate for ages 10 and over.

Copyright © 2001 American Girl, LLC. Reproduced with permission

GRG WEEK 6
Respect Essentials

☆ **The Basics Of Respect ....**
- ✓ Have Self-Respect
- ✓ Listen To Your Gut
- ✓ Set Boundaries
- ✓ Speak Up
- ✓ Build Relationships
- ✓ Fight For Equality
- ✓ Get Help

☆ **Your Rights – You've Got A Right To ....**
- ✓ Feel Like You Belong!
- ✓ Feel Like An Equal!
- ✓ Figure Out You!
- ✓ Listen To Your True Feelings!
- ✓ Be Different & Individual!
- ✓ Feel & Be Safe!
- ✓ Be Independent!
- ✓ Follow Your Passions!
- ✓ BE YOU!

☆ **Your Choices ....**
- ✓ How You Look & Dress
- ✓ How You Feed, Think About, & Take Care Of Your Body
- ✓ How You Treat Others
- ✓ How You Meet Your Obligations
  Ex: schoolwork, housework, keeping dates with friends
- ✓ How You Deal When Things Don't Work Out The Way You Want

From: Macavinta, Courtney and Vander Pluym, Andrea. *Respect: A Girl's Guide to Getting Respect & Dealing When Your Line is Crossed*. Minneapolis: Free Spirit Publishing, 2005. Reprinted with permission

Help Us Improve!!

GRG WEEK 6

Romantic Relationships & Review

What 3 Ideas Or Activities Did You Like Best This Week?

1.

2.

3.

Anything We Should Cut? Or Improve?

1.

2.

3.

Other Comments? Your Ideas Help Us A Lot!! Thanks!

GRG WEEK 6
Girls' Respect Groups Wrap Up
Whole Program Comments

1. Overall, I liked Girls' Respect Group

❏ A Lot ❏ Pretty Much ❏ Neutral ❏ Not So Much ❏ Not

2. What 3 ideas or things did you learn that have been most useful to you?

_____
_____
_____

3. What activities did you enjoy the most?

_____
_____
_____

4. Which activities did you enjoy least?

_____
_____
_____

5. How did you like ....

Activity	Liked It	Didn't Like	Tell Us More - Why?
Icebreakers			
The Book			
Videos			
Discussion			
Journal			
Homework			
Snacks			
Other Ideas			

GRG WEEK 6
Girls' Respect Groups Wrap Up

6. What will you do or are you doing differently since starting this group?

_____
_____
_____

7. What would you tell other girls who want to join or start a Girls' Respect Group?

_____
_____
_____

8. Anything else you'd like to tell us?

_____
_____
_____

Girls' Respect Groups: Keep It Going!

Thank You So Much For Making
Girls' Respect Group
So Great!!

Keep GRG Going On Your Own:
Read, Meet & Talk
Be Strong & Kind

Be Each Other's Friends
Take Care Of & Support Each Other
Ask Yourself: *Would A Friend Do This?*

Treat Yourself Like Your Own Best Friend
Be True To Yourself

**Be Proud Of Who You Are,
What You've Learned & Where You're Going**

We're Proud Of You !!

CHAPTER 13
Tips For Running Groups Smoothly

We'd like to pass on a few tips that have helped us a lot, from our hands-on experience running GRGs. We give them to you to shorten your learning curve and help you **run your most successful GRGs now!**

Don't Play Favorites. You're going to like some girls more and some girls less – just like life. But your job as a Leader means you have to be bigger than that, and you need to run your GRG evenhandedly & fairly, with encouragement and room for all to grow (Leaders, too!). You need to be nice to **everyone**! Find kind ways to say that you disagree with someone's viewpoint. "You know, that hasn't been my experience", or "That's how I thought about it, until this happened to me..." (& then tell the story), or "What's your experience on that one?" (to the group), or "Can you explain more?" are all good ways to encourage a girl to rethink or enlarge her views. If everyone jumps on a girl for her opinion, that's the quickest way to make her feel defensive and close her mind to change. We encourage the group to listen and learn from each other.

Facial Expressions

Be Aware Of Your Facial Expressions. Especially when someone says something you disagree with, practice the self-control not to let it show on your face. This is a special challenge during the teen years. Hint: If your parents are warning you about your eye-rolling during family "discussions", that's a **big hint** that you need to work on your facial self-control for GRG (this will help you *big time* in your family discussions, too). For example, I've realized that I often frown when I'm thinking or listening hard, which people could easily misinterpret as being angry or judgmental, and that would be the *opposite* of what I meant to convey.

Be Aware Of Personality Differences In The Group. Some girls (& Leaders) are introverts, some extroverts. Extroverts usually speak up sooner, and their stronger personalities can dominate a group, crowding out the participation of more

Dare To Be Different

introverted girls. Watch for this. This is where having 2 Leaders is really helpful. The Leader who's **not** leading the current activity can observe this much more easily and can help re-balance the activity by calling for others to add their opinions. This is something useful for Leaders to talk about in their Leaders' meetings or conversations between weekly GRG sessions. This can be one of the most challenging aspects of running a group. Experienced adult public speakers struggle with this, too. It's a continuing learning opportunity.

Set The Stage In Week 1 For Smooth Groups. Be clear from the start that you want everyone to feel comfortable to contribute, and that you know some girls will reach that comfort stage sooner than others. Ask everyone to help out with this, to be aware when they (or another girl) might be hogging the conversation a bit, and look for ways to involve everyone. By the way, it's normal for Leaders to feel a little nervous before Week 1, too. It helps the girls relax when they know you're feeling the same butterflies!

Snack. Girls have told us, time and again, that the snack was one of their favorite parts of GRG. There's a good reason for this. Our bodies and brains work **much** better when we give them some fuel. Giving the girls a healthy snack at the start of GRG gets their energy levels back up after a busy day at school. The fact that we insist on healthy snacks sends an important message that eating right is another form of respect, **respect for your body**.

Supplying the snack is usually someone else's responsibility. Our role is to be really clear with whoever's supplying the snack about what a healthy snack looks like. Don't just say "healthy snack". Be specific, as we described earlier, in Chapter 5, *How To Set Up & Run A GRG*. It's so important that we are mentioning it here, too. Let's put it this way: you **do not** want your girls and Leaders lying on the table at GRG because they don't have the mental or physical energy to participate!

Icebreakers. We start most weeks with an icebreaker. GRG builds trust in the group, and some of these icebreakers are trust-based games, allowing the girls to build bonds and share a little bit with each other before they open up and share their deeper thoughts, feelings, and problems.

Full Group Discussions: Some "How To"s & Tips

The most important and challenging aspect of running GRG is knowing how to spark and run a discussion. This involves thought and preparation, for both the content and the flow between Leaders, before you reach the meeting table.

✬ **Meet with your Co-Leader or talk on the phone before every meeting.** Even a few minutes makes a huge difference for running a smooth group. This is true even when you're an experienced GRG Leader. Refreshing your memory of the lesson content and dividing up responsibility for leading each activity really pays off in looking smooth and professional. Several activities ask the Leaders to share stories from their own experience. Preparing them in your prep session will help the group run smoothly, and also make sure you pick a story that's appropriate for 6th Graders!

✬ **Think about and prepare interesting stories about ... you.** Yes, you. The girls love to hear about you & your stories more than anything else. You are what they strive to be – a teen. They'll analyze, copy, & critique your every move. Sharing respectful stories about yourself helps preteens plan for how they'll handle similar situations. **Sharing your mistakes, too, shows you're not perfect and, way more important, what you learned & what you did different the next time.** Really, thanks for sharing!

✬ **Keep the content PG Rated (appropriate) for 6th Grade.** Even if you have a *great* story that emphasizes *all* of the *7 Respect Basics*, if it involves the party you went to last weekend, or it involves more mature activities, you might want to skip it. We don't want 11 year olds crashing a high school party because you made it sound cool.

✬ **Discuss, don't lecture.** Even though Leaders are crucial to GRG, it's not all about us. Our job is to make a space for the girls to talk. **Ask lots of questions, then let the girls answer 1st.** Encourage many answers, then help shape the discussion by adding extra ideas or stories, from the book or from your own experience. Keep it casual and friendly, a discussion where everyone contributes. If you're wondering if you're lecturing or discussing, look at the group. If the girls are falling asleep, you can bet you are lecturing!

✬ **Maintain encouraging eye contact.** This helps you connect with the girls. If you look at them while they speak (smiling, not frowning), they'll know you're interested in what they have to say. How do you think someone might feel if you just stare off into space while they talk? That strong connection allows girls to feel safe enough to try out new ideas, too.

Change Your World…Be Seen…Be Heard…Be Proud!!!

"When someone shows you who they are, believe them"

... *Maya Angelou*

Tips For Running Groups Smoothly

Transition Zones: When & How To Move On

When To Move On. It's not always clear when to move on to the next topic. Adult teachers struggle with this one, too. Each week is fully packed, and although we've left time for discussion, every group is different. Here are a few ideas.

Keeping Track Of Time Is The Best Strategy. Preparation helps. Look at the time markings for each activity on the Lesson Plans & pencil in the real finishing time for each activity. **Keep a watch on the desk.** That way you can monitor the time discreetly.

- ✡ **If your group is intensely interested in one topic, it's respectful to the group to spend more time.** You may have to adjust other activities. Listen to your gut. If it feels like it's time to keep going or to move on, it probably is.

- ✡ **Avoid abrupt transitions.** Sometimes, a group can get very deep into a topic or it can bring up strong emotions (sometimes both). Even when you have to move on, it's important to have some emotional closure before doing so. For example, ask for 3 suggestions or ideas to resolve it or move it forward before the next meeting. Then make yourself a note and make sure that you open next week's meeting with a **brief** follow-up. Arrive early & you can discuss it as you set up the room if it feels right.

How To Move On. It takes some finesse to change the topic – experienced teachers and speakers find it a challenge, too. Practice helps! Use these ideas to help.

- ✡ **Choose a respectful hand signal for "time" or "quiet".** Set this up with the girls in Week 1 (Activity 3). When you run over time, or things are getting out of hand, show the symbol (for example, T for Time). If this doesn't work, sit quietly and wait. Proceed when you have their attention.

- ✡ **Change it up – take a motion break.** Sometimes, moving on to a new discussion topic isn't enough to energize or focus the girls. They've had a long day at school, and you're all that's standing between them and home! You can switch gears by doing something physical. Keep a list of 5 min activities for handy reference. Act out a respect story, do a role play (follow up on an activity from previous weeks), use an activity from the book, or stretch & jump. Make sure to get the group back on track after 5 min (start at 4!) – it could be a challenge!

Those are some of our favorite tips. Let us know yours!

CHAPTER 14
Special Situations

Be flexible. As you run more groups, you may find that you need to alter lesson plans to make them flow better or to accommodate the special needs of participants. This is OK. Be open to change. **Let us know how you've changed the program to make it work better** and we'll share that info with the GRG network!

For example, **a Leader or participant may have a physical or learning disability. Our job, as Leaders and as human beings, is to make her feel welcome and to help her be (& feel that she's) a full part of GRG.** For a girl with a physical disability, icebreakers with lots of physical activity may need to be modified. Flipped the other way, it would be an awful example of disrespect if we, the champions of respect, showed disrespect to a girl with differences. **In the big picture, we all have strengths & weaknesses, even without a diagnosis or label. We can only grow when people make room for us & help us.** What if our parents took one look at us as babies and said, "Whoa, look at how small & helpless & stupid she is – never mind!" What if our teachers said, "Wow, what an ignorant & uneducated child. Why bother?" **Our lives are enriched by the willingness of others, who know more, can do more, or have more life experience, to stop and make time to teach us, help us, and pick us up when we stumble.**

Another example might be a girl with autism, who finds it difficult to make social connections. She may read social cues very poorly and as a result, could become an easy target of bullying & girls' relational exclusion. Membership in a girls' group would be especially helpful to a girl like this. This girl, like everyone, has her own unique intelligence – she may just have difficulties expressing herself in the "typical" ways.

Don't pre-judge. Be creative about solutions. For example, kids with autism, who find it difficult to make eye contact or to speak smoothly, are often liberated by using a computer. Speaking through a keyboard, you may find a deeply articulate and thoughtful friend. Whatever form her participation takes, for this girl to know that she is now a member of a protective group of girlfriends as she walks down the frequently perilous school hallways is a huge support.

For ideas on how to alter a lesson plan, ask the girl what works for her, or what she feels capable of. She knows herself better than anyone else! Ask the group for ideas. Often, they've gone to school together for years, and they may have great ideas.

Remember, **every GRG is different**. It's made up of different girls, with individual personalities, interests, and traits. Don't stunt that individuality. Embrace it, and **allow the group to take on its own unique form.** That's what makes Girls' Respect Groups so interesting!

> "Our deepest fear is not that we are inadequate.
> Our deepest fear is that we are powerful beyond measure.
> It is our light, not our darkness, that most frightens us.
> We ask ourselves, who am I to be brilliant, gorgeous,
> talented, & fabulous? Actually, who are you not to be?
> You are a child of God.
> Your playing small doesn't serve the world.
> There's nothing enlightened about shrinking
> so that other people won't feel insecure around you.
> We are all meant to shine, as children do.
> We are born to make manifest the glory of God that is within us.
> It's not just in some of us, it's in everyone.
> And as we let our own light shine,
> we unconsciously give other people permission to do the same.
> As we are liberated from our own fear,
> our presence automatically liberates others"
>
> ... Marianne Williamson

CHAPTER 15
Handle This! Awkward Moments & How To Survive Them

Here's where we give you a leg up on some of the awkward moments that can, and probably will, come up in GRG if you run enough of them. Most are nothing earth-shattering, but it helps to have a few tips on how to deal with these situations. With experience, you'll get better at handling problems. Don't worry, you're not expected to be the expert or magically solve the problem. Usually what's needed is a kind heart, a sympathetic ear, some patience, & knowing when an adult's help might be useful.

HANDLE THIS!
A Girl Starts Crying

Sticky Situation!

Suggestion: This is when having 2 Leaders *really* comes in handy. One Leader can take the girl who's upset aside (find a private place). Take time to calm her down, ask her what's wrong, and how you can help. Depending on the issue, you can make some helpful suggestions and bring her back into GRG (highly recommended, so GRG friends can offer support), or you can call a parent, if needed.

Sometimes, the girl who's crying or upset doesn't need advice or a solution to the problem; she just needs someone to listen to what's bothering her. Make sure to listen for a long time before jumping in with ideas. Ask open-ended questions: "Is there more?", "What happened then?", "How'd you feel?".

Don't get flipped out if someone starts to cry. Crying is just one of your body's normal ways to release tension. That said, if crying (or yelling) is the *only* thing we know how to do when we're under stress or upset, that's a signal we need to learn a few more stress release & conflict resolution skills. GRG will be a good place to start, and there are lots of resources we can refer to for extra learning. See the Resources section at the end of the book for more ideas.

Remember: Handle this with care. When a girl is clearly upset, she needs some additional attention. Don't try to minimize her discomfort or feelings. Hear out everything she has to say before offering advice. The problem may be as small as the surfacing of a sad memory, or it could be as big as a group of kids planning to beat her up after school the next day.

HANDLE THIS!
Some Girls Can't Focus Or Everyone's Talking At Once

Sticky Situation!

Suggestion: Having a signal to remind everyone when it's time to calm down or stop talking is very helpful. In Week 1, set this up with the girls so that everyone agrees and feels like they had a part in the decision. We've used: hold up a hand, hold up a peace sign, or make a "T" for Time Out. If you use your signal & girls are still talking, don't wrestle with the group for control. Wait until everyone has reasonably settled down before continuing. Remind everyone that it's not respectful to talk over each other. Even worse, we might run out of time & not get to some of the activities!

Remember: GRG is not actual school and you don't want the girls to think of GRG as something they have to do. Don't try to punish the girls or single them out meanly in front of everyone. If our earlier suggestions don't bring enough order to continue, usually a simple, "Kiara, do you need a moment outside to calm down?" or "Lindsay, would you like to step out for a quick drink?" should suffice. Thankfully, GRG girls are there by choice and will really take your words to heart because they all want to talk about their favorite things and join in the discussions.

HANDLE THIS!
The "Mean Girl" Doesn't Come To GRG

Sticky Situation!

Suggestion: This happens often. In real life, the bully (or problem child or adult) *rarely* shows up and says "Hi, I think I'm causing a problem. Can you help me change? I really want to work on it." (Wouldn't that be great??) But this girl, and often a few girls around her, can be making life pretty miserable for everyone in her path. In fact, she often makes her "friends" miserable, too. **You may think this girl isn't part of GRG, but you'd be wrong. She or, more accurately, her bad behavior, comes to GRG every week, even if she's not there.**

GRG is the *perfect* place to discuss these issues, out of the glare and emotional intensity. It's a chance to safely, sanely, & rationally discuss & problem-solve, with a subset of the cast of characters, under the experience & guidance of the teen Leaders. Fortunately, there are usually

members of both (or all) cliques around the table at GRG, so it's a beautiful opportunity for both sets of girls to think, hear, & understand the impact of their behavior on each other, **and on themselves.**

Here's the life lesson: *We can only change ourselves, no matter how bad someone else's behavior is around us.* But we have far more power than we realize, to set boundaries, to make choices, to walk away, to not let our buttons be pushed, to see someone for who they really are. Note: If this is a physical safety issue, read on about BIG PROBLEMS.

Put simply, if the environment around the "mean girl" changes, she will change, too. When people stop responding to her demands, and when they don't care to be her servant, her power base weakens or evaporates (It's perfectly OK to be friends when she's friendly – don't bully her!).

Here's what we mean: Members of 2 cliques were part of GRG. We'll call them the "You Can't Be Our Friend" group (YCBOF) and the "Please, Please Be Our Friend" group (PPBOF). The ringleader of YCBOF was not part of GRG – no surprise there. One girl from YCBOF, trying to be friendly to all, was caught in the middle, in trouble with her "queen bee" YCBOF group for talking or hanging out with girls from PPBOF. This in-the-middle girl was also on the spot with the PPBOF girls, trying to defend or rationalize the mean girls' YCBOF behavior. She also had to confront her own, flip-flop behavior (nice to you when we're alone, freeze you out when I'm with my YCBOF girls). Talk about a tough situation!

The YCBOF girls even made the other kids call them "The Populars"! No kidding! When our Leaders heard that, they saw a "**Stop Everything!**" opportunity to encourage the PPBOF girls at the table to *think about what they were doing*. Why are you giving someone else so much power? Why are you giving away your own power? Why would you want to be friends with people who treat you so badly????

Step #1: Stop calling them "The Populars" – to their faces **AND** to yourselves. And just like that, things shifted. Did it magically solve the whole problem that minute? Of course not. But it opened the door to change.

Remember: Life's not perfect. It takes time for situations to get bad, and months (or years) to work it out. Some things you can't really fix (time helps). We need the resilience to roll with the ups & downs of life and still be our best selves, even (especially) when people around us aren't "behaving". If we can only be happy when everyone around us is playing by our rules, how often can we be happy – 1% of the time? We want more power and personal control in our lives than that! Besides, wouldn't life be small & boring if there were no drama at all??!!

> **HANDLE THIS!**
> **2 Girls Get Into A Big Argument**

Sticky Situation!

Suggestion: We encourage all girls to express their opinions. We want and expect differences and even some conflicts that will get worked out (respectfully) in GRG. This is not what we mean. We're talking about when the talking escalates to yelling or name-calling, or even the threat of a physical fight (yes, girls do that, too). You'll know as a Leader when it's approaching the "Whoa" point. This is when you really need to jump right in before someone gets too angry or hurt. "Girls, we need to calm down right now," or "Whoa, everyone stop and take a breath," are good openers to stop the argument. Make sure it stops *immediately* and that the Leaders remain in control (note: if you can't, then it's time to call an adult – NOW!). This has never happened to us in GRG, but we've all seen it happen in other environments – on the playground, at camp, at the movies, at parties, so it's best to be prepared and know what to do, just in case.

Give everybody a 5 min break, to help re-set their body chemistry. Eating or drinking water or juice helps. Then, when things have cooled a bit, ask if the girls need a mediator or if they could use your help. Ask if they can leave the problem for right now and suggest that you talk with them after the group is finished, so everyone can get through the week's material. If the girls are agreeable to that, thank them very much for the maturity it takes to be able to do that. If they clearly can't put their problems aside, if really necessary, 1 Leader could take both girls aside while the group is still running. We really don't recommend this option, because nobody left in the group will be able to concentrate on anything else but what's happening outside the room. Use your judgement whether this problem is best solved by the whole group together. You may get nothing else done that week, but it may be worth it to set a great example of successfully tackling difficult issues.

If you decide to go with an after-group discussion, if you feel you can help as mediator, encourage the girls to re-start the conversation, with the idea of hearing each other and working to a solution. Hear both sides of the argument, and handle everything fairly and treat both girls kindly, even (*especially*) if you think 1 girl was "wrong". It's a real talent to be able to help 2 people who've been very upset with each other to reconsider, take responsibility, and to each apologize for her part of things getting out of control (that applies to both sides!). They may still disagree at the end & that's ok!

Remember: Handle this situation with all your tact, and never flip out yourself. This is a great chance to teach mutual respect, even when a disagreement occurs. Help guide the girls to their own solution, practicing the art of respect, even in their distress.

HANDLE THIS!
The Group Becomes Listless

Sticky Situation!

Suggestion: Sometimes it's hard to sit still after a long day of school, even if you've had a break & a snack. Most meetings just fly by, but it helps to change it up after an hour. Plan an extra icebreaker or a 2 min physical, stand-up-&-stretch activity. If your week's activities include role playing or another kinetic activity, it's great to time it for that 60 min "dead zone".

Remember: This problem can't always be avoided, but having a nutritious snack, an energetic icebreaker, and moving on from topic to topic really helps keep the conversation alive (we've learned to move on while the conversation is still good).

HANDLE THIS!
The Group Gangs Up On 1 Girl

Sticky Situation!

Suggestion: Often, members of 2 or more different social groups come to GRG. Sometimes those groups have problems getting along, or there are problems with girls' relational exclusion or bullying. Eventually, those problems make their way to GRG, even if they don't directly involve the specific GRG members. Don't worry, this is good! This is a measure of how much trust and safety you've built in the group. Tell the girls this, too.

When girls want to describe a problem that involves naming names, we teach them from the 1st week not to use people's real names when talking about problems. Somehow, using made-up names seems to de-personalize the problem and allows everyone to discuss it more even-handedly, and, hopefully, see things a bit from the other side, as well. Let's be real – nobody's fooling anybody, and everybody in the group usually knows exactly who they're talking about (only the Leaders haven't met them, if they're outside the GRG group). There have been some hilarious moments while the group struggles to come up with "the right" fake name for someone in a social drama. "No, that's not a good name!"

Behind the renaming giggles can lurk some seriously disrespectful behavior and some very hurt feelings (remember "The Populars"?). Leaders, be careful. You can end up with 5 girls verbally ganging up on 1 girl who is trying to defend herself or her friends for past misbehavior. When this starts to happen, stress that ganging up is not tolerated, not fair, & most importantly, very disrespectful. If you want someone to understand or be open to your point of view, you have to talk to them in ways that they can really hear it, not by beating them over the head. These discussions of outside problems are pivotal moments, where 1 girl can suddenly see that her (or her friend's) treatment of another girl has been rude, hurtful, dismissive, or belittling. In the right supportive environment, these "ah ha" moments can provide powerful encouragement and the 1st steps to change.

Remember: Not every problem has a solution where 2 girls go skipping off into the sunset, best friends holding hands. **It's important to remember that we don't have to be best friends with everybody. We don't even have to *like* everybody. We *do* have to make a place for everybody, and we must be able to get along with & work & play with everybody.**

HANDLE THIS!
A BIG PROBLEM Is Revealed

Sticky Situation!

Suggestion: It's awesome that the girls trust you enough to tell you about a BP. A Big Problem can mean someone is in danger and something needs to be done immediately. What's a BP? You'll know it when you hear it. Our friend Carolyn, a high school teacher, said, "Yeah, it's when you hear about it and your stomach drops." Some examples of a BP include:

✫ Plans for a kid to be attacked, beaten up, or hurt in the near future

✫ Stories of physical or sexual abuse

✫ Worries of a kid feeling or acting suicidal

✫ Evidence of self-destructive behavior – cutting, over-drinking, over-drugging, over-sexing (or too early)

Take the girl or girls aside. Learn everything you can. Who? What? Where? When? Why? How? This is one reason why there is an Adult Advisor, as well as a Teacher Contact from the school, and this would be an appropriate instance to have them directly involved.

Remember: The less time there is until the BP occurs or occurs again, the faster you need to act by telling a parent, teacher, principal, maybe even the police. Do not go around telling everyone about the big drama. Be a compassionate, responsible, trustworthy Leader.

HANDLE THIS!
You Want To Kick Someone Out Of The Group

Sticky Situation!

Suggestion: Like we said, you're not going to love everyone, and some people's personalities can really clash with each other or with yours! It's possible you could have 1 girl who's hogging all the air time, or being disrespectful to others. Bad behavior patterns that started long before GRG aren't going to magically disappear just because you wish it so.

There's a lot you can do (and probably have done) to prevent this problem. First, participation in GRG is voluntary – nobody's being forced to be here. Next, descriptions of GRG and registration letters went home before GRG started, spelling out our expectations about the girls' responsibilities. These were read and signed by all girls and their parents, so we hope everybody's on the same page. Last, Leaders did a good job setting the stage in Week 1 for a smooth-running GRG, when everybody talked about the guidelines for respect for each other that we expect in all our meetings.

Problem children are pretty evident from Week 1. Don't let it build. Intervene early, gently, and often. Remind girls of their obligations to be good citizens of GRG. If you have to start every GRG with a recap of our guidelines for respectful treatment of each other, it's worth it. Some groups need to be run a little tighter than others. Keep the (kind & respectful) pressure on, keep reminding them of the guidelines, and keep expecting people to grow into your good expectations. Stay positive and in control, without being controlling – a delicate balance. Meet with your Co-Leader for a snack after group meetings and let it all out with each other! Think of it as a good test of *your* self-control!

Remember: People (kids & adults) often act the *least* loveable when they need love the *most*. By keeping a girl like this in the group, when you most feel like tossing her *out*, know that you are doing something kind & special, making a place for someone who desperately needs love and acceptance, *especially* when she's going about it the completely wrong way. As Leaders, you provide yet another example of how we make space for others *even while* encouraging and insisting on change.

Be Patient

love & acceptance

HANDLE THIS!
A 6th Grade Parent Objects To Respect's Chapters On Dating & Sex

Sticky Situation!

Suggestion: This would be a good thing to hand over to your Adult Advisor, but you can say it just the way they would. Tell them this is what we told the girls in Week 1:

In 6 weeks, we don't have time to read and discuss the whole book. **Respect** is written for middle and high school girls. For middle schoolers, we are not going over the chapters on dating & sex – most girls aren't ready for or interested in that yet. But we love the book, and we tell the girls to hold on to it, because when they're interested and ready to learn more, we really like what the book has to say about the "yucky stuff", too.

We find that **Respect** can open a conversation between a parent and child, or at the least, reassure a parent that their child is getting a respect-based reference book, even if the parent or the child isn't ready for a face-to-face talk.

Remember: Be respectful towards the parent, even if they have a different view of the value of educating their kids about "adult" topics. If you have any concern about having this conversation with an adult, give the parent a big smile and say "Absolutely let me pass you over to our Adult Advisor." And then do so, either directly, or by taking the parent's contact info and assuring them that the Advisor will call them.

HANDLE THIS!
A 6th Grade Girl Asks A Teen Leader About Her Sex Life

Suggestion: This can be an uncomfortable moment (wait till you have kids!), so it's best to prepare in advance to handle personal questions gracefully. Pointed questions could be on any topic: sex, dating, drug use, drinking, lying (for example: cheating on a test or lying to your parents). Mostly, the girls are just intensely curious about every aspect of your life, so think of it as questioning based on admiration. As a Leader, we are grateful for all that you **do** share with the girls, but that doesn't mean your life must be a completely open book.

Here's one way to handle it, but find words that feel authentic to you. "Well, it's not really about me specifically or any one of us. Sex (drinking, drugs, etc) involves some thinking before you do it. These can be private decisions, and it's ok to have some parts of us that we keep a little private."

150 Girls' Respect Groups

"Some of these activities can be really risky or even deadly if they're done the wrong way or at the wrong time. And sometimes we have to make these decisions under pressure, so it's best to think it through in advance. You want to make good decisions so you can look back and feel happy that you respected yourself. We each must make our own best decision and we might each make different decisions. That's ok, too."

"Girls' Respect Group is just a start on these topics. You'll want to read and talk more as you get older. We need to find the right balance between openness and everyone's need for some privacy. I'll answer your questions as best I can, but I might also say, 'Oh, that's gone over my privacy line'."

Remember: Filter your answer through what's appropriate for a 6th Grade audience!

CHAPTER 16
Continuing Training & Growth For Leaders

In life, success comes from continual learning. We can improve, no matter where we start. The same is true for GRG Leaders. We start off great, but we're not stopping there! Even after you've run a couple of GRGs and know the ropes, there's always more to learn. Stay in touch with your GRG network between groups. It's a positive presence in your life, a place where you can always turn for growth and encouragement.

Success Is A Process Of Continual Learning

After running a real, live GRG, it's understandable to want the great experience to continue. We sure did! The friendly, open environment with teen girls helping preteen girls is truly something special. Plus, the friendships between Co-Leaders become really strong & these are friends that you'll want to keep! This is why you'll want to use some of these ideas for continuing training, even for Leaders who have already run several Girls' Respect Groups (ourselves included!).

What To Do After Your 6 Week GRG Or Between GRGs

- ✪ **Have a wrap up meeting with GRG Leaders and your Adult Advisor(s)** right after Week 6 of every GRG. These big picture meetings are great for discussing what you've learned. Every group is different – you'll learn every time. Ask yourselves what went well and where to make changes for next time, both to the program and with individual Leaders. Get feedback from the Teacher Contact at the school to bring to this meeting. Do this while you're still fresh from GRG and the memories are clear.

- ✪ **Identify the need for additional training.** For example, you might want to bring in Children's Aid for an informational workshop for Leaders. Leaders can identify areas for personal improvement.

- ✪ **Take some time off from GRG.** We appreciate all the time and heart you've just poured into your GRG. It's also good to take a breather and focus on other things for a bit. Life is all about balance! Time off helps you keep it fresh and grow as a Leader.

- ✪ **Be respectful in everyday life.** Remain conscious of your role as a teen mentor and leader, an example to younger kids and to your peers. Count to 10 before you flip out in public, or at home. Try not to gossip or be around other gossips (better yet, stop others from gossiping). There are lots of little things that spell R-E-S-P-E-C-T every day. It's not just what we do in GRG.

- ✦ **Notice everyday examples of respect and disrespect in action.** TV shows, magazine ads, politics, videos, and movies provide lots of interesting ideas. Take some notes on good examples to use next time you run a GRG.

OK, Your Battery's All Charged Up & You're Ready! What Else Can You Do?

- ✦ **Run another GRG at the school where you just finished, for another group of girls.** Capture that enthusiasm! If you have enough Leaders, you can run several groups at the same time. Looking into the future, set a goal to run 3 more (or 6 or double your number of) GRGs next year!

- ✦ **Work with the same Co-Leader for several GRGs.** Keeping the same leadership team helps you get comfortable with each other, build stronger bonds, and run better groups. With experience, you get better at handing off the discussion and transitioning from the leader to the observer role. You can play off each other's stories and even develop stories together.

- ✦ **After building a strong co-leading style, it's also good to work with other Leaders, to expand your knowledge** and learn other styles and techniques. Pair a more experienced or stronger Leader with a newer or less advanced Leader. Both will become well-rounded Leaders.

- ✦ **Stir up enthusiasm and find 6th Grade participants for GRGs at local middle schools.** GRG Leaders can speak at middle school assemblies, school council meetings, or extracurricular activities. Your Adult Advisor can make the initial contact with the Principal or a teacher.

- ✦ **Find & train new Leaders.** Talk to Grade 10 girls at high school assemblies, after school activities, high school club days & community centers in your city. You'll be a great advocate for GRG, now that you've led some groups. You'll be a great trainer, too, helping the next group of young women become GRG Leaders. We can help teens take action and make a difference! Keep your eyes open for potential Leaders. You never know where you might meet a great Leader. Get recruiting!

- ✦ **Go back to schools where you've run GRGs and meet with the girls.** See how they're doing. This is a great way to get ideas for keeping past participants involved. Bring handouts describing our GRG online community and parental permission slips for the girls to sign up. Ask the Principal or your Teacher Contact if or when they'd like to run another GRG.

Dream Big & Reach For The Stars

- ✧ **Meet with GRG Leaders and Advisors in your community, town, or city.** Find out about girls at different schools. What are their issues? What are they into? How do these GRGs compare to yours? Make plans to run more GRGs in your shared community. Expand the GRG network!

- ✧ **Take it to the next level. Connect with teen Leaders in other provinces, states, and countries.** Attend leadership camps, regional and national girls' workshops and retreats, and participate in community or volunteer activities.

Contact us! We have a ton of ideas to keep you in the GRG mind space! Send us your creative ideas and we'll pass them along to other GRG Leaders.

What If It's Not Working? Leaders Who Need To Improve

We all need improvement, but sometimes it just doesn't work out and we have to ask a teen to step aside as a Leader. We've never had this happen, but you have to be prepared that it might. Here's the time to exercise **all** your respect muscles! A big part of respect is being nice, **especially** in uncomfortable situations or when you have to give someone bad news.

Not everyone will be ready to run a GRG right after training. Some need extra practice and experience before running a real, live GRG. They may not have had enough background experience or maybe their facilitation skills need a little work. This is a good time for the Adult Advisor to give gentle feedback, with clear expectations for where a teen needs to grow and improve. Find ways to keep these teens involved with GRG while they're growing into their role as Leaders.

Some Leaders May Need To Improve... With A Little Help

How To Give Good Feedback

Positive & Objective Feedback

Here's the tough part: How do you tell someone that you don't like what they're doing, without crushing their spirit? This is a challenge whether the feedback comes from a co-leading peer or from your Adult Advisor.

We want our feedback to be fair & effective. To be helpful, it should be as objective as possible, not just personal preferences. Having an evaluation checklist for each training activity encourages all participants, Co-Leaders, and Adult Advisors to give simple feedback on a Leader's performance in all activities. That way, Leaders get constructive criticism ("Yeas & Nays") along the way. We all have our strengths and weaknesses, and it's helpful to get objective suggestions for improvement. It's good to know early, too, so you can work on it throughout training. It would be disrespectful to say nothing until you spring a terrible "You suck" on someone at the end. Encourage leaders to self-assess & set growth goals, too. You can modify & use the Leaders' Training Feedback Forms from Chapter 4.

Here are some tips for kind-hearted, useful feedback:

- **Be kind**. Keep your tone of voice neutral and non-accusatory. Think how you would feel if you were in her shoes. Be gentle. Above all, be respectful!

- **Be honest and clear**. Say what isn't working and why. Give a specific example. Don't use "You always…" or "You never…".

- **Give support and ideas for change**. Use "What if we…" or "Do you think you could…" as lead-ins. Use the examples of what isn't working and offer some suggestions for how to handle it differently.

- **Give some time to improve and set a meeting date for the next evaluation**. That way, you're both aware of the time frame required for improvement. We suggest 1 or 2 weeks, depending on the opportunities available for practice.

- **Has she improved?** If she hasn't, politely tell her that she just isn't great for the job right now. If she has, congratulate her, but let her know that she needs to **keep it up**!

- **If you choose not to continue working with her, keep in touch**, and let her know that if she puts in the effort, she could be a great Leader in the future.

Don't give up on young women who aren't quite ready now. They will grow, and when they do, they'll be amazing Leaders. The fact that they want to help others speaks volumes. Even if they don't turn out to be a GRG Leader, going through GRG training can help start someone on their own path to maturity. GRG helps girls in many ways!

Stay Positive & Keep Growing

For GRG Leaders, every day presents an opportunity for knowledge and growth. Sometimes it's a small thing, like going out of our way to help someone who really needs it, that contributes the most to our own evolution as leaders and human beings. Look for these moments, both big and small.

The future is limitless for GRG graduates – Leaders, Participants, & Advisors. Everyone you touch is enriched and encouraged to grow, by the respect you demonstrate for yourself and those around you. Keep it up! We can't wait to see how you change the world!

CHAPTER 17
Stay In Touch!

We hope that you are now as pumped as we are about the **power of respect and the huge ability of women to help each other.** We truly believe that by teaching each other about the value of respect, supporting each other and staying strong, building up the GRG network, and insisting on respect for all, we are building the foundation for a worldwide end to disrespect. Imagine getting along in schools and workplaces without bullying or being bullied. **Women can make this change!** (and men need to help!)

It feels like it was only yesterday when we started the GRG program, but in fact many hours, laughs, dilemmas, and brainstorms have paved the way for this book. We are delighted to pass it on to you, and for you each to add your own personal touch, your own knowledge and experience, to keep GRG growing.

Please **stay in touch with us!** We want to hear about your branch of the GRG network. We want to hear about your successes, your challenges, your milestones, and your growing pains.

Thank you for all your hard work & your positive spirit!

You will be amazing leaders
& make a huge difference in this world!

With Love & Respect,

Lorna　　　　　　*Natalie*　　　　　　*Anne*

Lorna　　　　　　　Natalie　　　　　　　Anne

CHAPTER 18
Resources

RESPECT

Brashich, Audrey. *All Made Up: A Girl's Guide to Seeing Through the Celebrity Hype... and Celebrating Real Beauty*. New York: Walker & Company, 2006.

Harlan, Judith. *Girl Talk: Staying Strong, Feeling Good, and Sticking Together*. Markham, ON: Thomas Allen & Son Canada, 1997.

Macavinta, Courtney and Vander Pluym, Andrea. *Respect: A Girl's Guide to Getting Respect & Dealing When Your Line is Crossed*. Minneapolis: Free Spirit Publishing, 2005.

RespectRx.com

GirlsRespectGroups.com

BULLYING

Blumen, Lorna. "Bystanders to Children's Bullying: The Importance of Leadership by 'Innocent Bystanders'". In Riggio, R, Chaleff, I, and Lipman-Blumen, J. (eds). *The Art of Followership: How Great Followers Create Great Leaders and Organizations*. San Francisco: Jossey-Bass, 2008.

Coloroso, Barbara. *The Bully, the Bullied, and the Bystander*. Toronto: Harper Collins, 2002.

Dellasega, Cheryl and Nixon, Charisse. *Girl Wars: 12 Strategies That Will End Female Bullying*. New York: Fireside, 2003.

Giannetti, Charlene and Sagarese, Margaret. *Cliques: 8 Steps to Help Your Child Survive the Social Jungle*. New York: Broadway Books, 2001.

Simmons, Rachel. *Odd Girl Out: The Hidden Culture of Aggression in Girls*. Orlando: Harcourt Inc, 2002.

Wiseman, Rosalind. *Queen Bees and Wannabes: Helping Your Daughter Survive Cliques, Gossip, Boyfriends, and Other Realities of Adolescence*. New York: Crown, 2002.

STRESS

Davies, Phillipa. *Thriving Under Stress*. London: DK Publishing, 2003.

Holyoke, Nancy, Watkins, Michelle and Maring, Therese. *A Smart Girl's Guide to Sticky Situations: How to Tackle Tricky, Icky Problems and Tough Times*. Middleton, WI: Pleasant Company Publications, 2002.

FRIENDSHIPS

Carey, Joely. *Staying Cool: Straightforward, No-Nonsense Advice to Girls on Dealing With Social Situations*. London: Axis Publishing Ltd, 2002.

Criswell, Patti. *A Smart Girl's Guide to Friendship Troubles*. Middleton, WI: Pleasant Company Publications, 2003.

Holyoke, Nancy. *A Smart Girl's Guide to Boys: Surviving Crushes, Staying True to Yourself, and Other Stuff*. Middleton, WI: Pleasant Company Publications, 2001.

ICEBREAKERS & GAMES

- **Body Beat.** Christine Stevens. UBDrumCircles.com
  - Rhythmical icebreakers with a deck of cards. Everybody plays the rhythm on their card, making a percussive symphony. Cool ways of working together wordlessly.

- **If You Had To Choose: A Fantasy Game About Priorities.** Choose Games, Inc. IfYouHadToChooseGame.com
  - **Note:** Many of these situations are about sex, so read the deck first, and edit appropriately. You can make up your own deck of discussion cards, too!

- **Daily Boosts In A Jar For Teens.** AttitudeMatters.com
  - Tools For Life: 101 Lessons For Getting Along
  - Gratitude For Teens: Daily Inspirations, 365 Reflections
  - Daily Dilemmas In A Jar: 101 Decisions To Think & Talk About

- **Circle Of Respect & Real Friends.** Board games from Franklin Learning Systems. FranklinLearning.com
  - FLS produces a wide range of educational board games on topics like respect, bullying prevention, and cooperation. Use the board or just use the cards for discussion!

Ordering Info

Online Orders:

Direct From Publisher:
- **CamberleyPress.com**

Online Booksellers:
- **Amazon.com**
- **Amazon.ca**
- **Chapters.Indigo.ca**

For Bulk Or Multiple Copy Orders, Contact:

- **CamberleyPress.com**
- **GirlsRespectGroups.com**

Printed in the United States
147388LV00002B/2/P